All Seasons Slow Cooker
Recipes for Horselovers

Volume 1

All Seasons Slow Cooker Recipes for Horselovers

Volume 1

Get out of the Kitchen and Into the Saddle in 15 minutes or Less

Debbie Overman

Debbie Overman
P.O. Box 390347
Anza, Ca. 92539
Contact: www.winterskymoonranch.com
Email: info@winterskymoonranch.com
Phone: 888.617.3177

ISBN 978-0-578-09836-4 soft cover
Library of Congress Number: 2011963600

Printed in the United States of America
This book is printed on acid-free paper.

On the cover: Debbie's Few Spot Appaloosa Stallion,
Winter's Skydancer

Contents

Soups & Stews............44

Beef............66

For my Mom and Dad ~ Thank you for sacrificing so much so that I could live my passions and dreams.

I am grateful to Chris who believed

For all of the horses who have shared their lives with me, and in doing so have become my greatest teachers: Biscuit (pony), Little Britches (Boob horse), Patrick's Poco, Twister, Sundance, Carousel Cowgirl (Mama), Magnum's Moon (Doodle), Elvis, Indigo, Sashay, Fabiana, Magic, Cherokee Sky, Cherokee Moon, Winters Skydancer, Blue Dog Moon, Winter's Medicinecrow, Epona's Moon, Sparkle Rose Dude (Hannah). Winter's Autumn Moon, Winter's Sparkling Rose, Winter's Ghostdancer, Grand Future and Aragorn.

Finally, to you who purchase this book: I hope that it helps to make your life easier so that you have the extra time you need to chase your dreams and pursue your passions.

Just A Horse

From time to time, people tell me, "lighten up, it's just a horse," or, "that's a lot of money for "just a horse." They don't understand the distance traveled, the time spent, or the costs involved for "just a horse."

Some of my proudest moments have come about with "just a horse." Many hours have passed and my only company was "just a horse," but I did not once feel slighted. Some of my saddest moments have been brought about by "just a horse," and in those days of darkness, the gentle touch of "just a horse" gave me comfort and reason to overcome the day.

If you, too, think it's "just a horse," then you will probably understand phrases like "just a friend," "just a sunrise," or "just a promise." "Just a horse" brings into my life the very essence of friendship, trust, and pure unbridled joy. "Just a horse" brings out the compassion and patience that make me a better person. Because of "just a horse" I will rise early, take long rides and look longingly to the future.

So for me and people like me, it's not "just a horse" but an embodiment of all the hopes and dreams of the future, the fond memories of the past, and the pure joy of the moment. "Just a horse" brings out what's good in me and diverts my thoughts away from myself and the worries of the day. I hope that someday they can understand that it's not "just a horse" but the thing that gives me humanity and keeps me from being "just a human."

So the next time you hear the phrase "just a horse" just smile, because they "just" don't understand. ~Anonymous

Breakfast

Breakfast Apple Cobbler

6 TART APPLES, CHOPPED
3 CUPS GRANOLA CEREAL
2 TABLESPOONS CINNAMON
3/4 CUP HONEY
2 TABLESPOONS MELTED BUTTER
PINCH OF NUTMEG
PINCH OF DRY GINGER
1/4 CUP CHOPPED WALNUTS

BUTTER SIDES & BOTTOM OF SLOW COOKER. POUR
GRANOLA, APPLES, CINNAMON, GINGER & HONEY INTO
BOWL, MIX TOGETHER. POUR INTO SLOW COOKER, DRIZZLE
WITH MELTED BUTTER, ADD NUTMEG. TOP WITH NUTS
WHEN SERVING.

COOK ON LOW 3-5 HOURS

SERVINGS: 4

Small children are convinced that ponies deserve to see the inside of the house. ~Maya Patel

BREAKFAST GRAINS & NUTS

1/2 CUP SHORT GRAIN BROWN RICE
1/2 CUP WASHED MILLET
1/2 CUP WASHED BARLEY
3.5 CUPS WATER
1 CUP CHOPPED DATES OR RAISINS
1 TEASPOON VANILLA
1 TEASPOON LEMON JUICE
1/2 TEASPOON GRATED GINGER
1 CUP NUTS, CHOPPED FINE

SET ASIDE NUTS. MIX ALL OTHER INGREDIENTS TOGETHER.

COOK ON LOW 5-6 HOURS, HIGH 3-4 HOURS. TOP WITH NUTS.

SERVINGS: 4

There is something about the outside of a horse that is good for the inside of a man. ~ Winston Churchill

EGG & HAM CASSEROLE

32 OZ. BAG FROZEN HASH BROWN POTATOES
1 POUND COOKED HAM, CUBED
3 SLICES BACON, COOKED & DICED
6 GREEN ONIONS, DICED
1 GREEN BELL PEPPER, DICED
1 ZUCCHINI, DICED
2 CUPS SHREDDED CHEESE
12 EGGS
1/2 CUP MILK
1/8 TEASPOON SALT
1/2 TEASPOON PEPPER
1 TABLESPOON OLIVE OIL

MIX ALL INGREDIENTS TOGETHER, EXCEPT HASH BROWNS
& CHEESE. PLACE ONE THIRD OF HASH BROWNS IN THE
BOTTOM OF GREASED SLOW COOKER. ADD ONE THIRD
EGG MIXTURE, & CHEESE. REPEAT LAYERS ENDING WITH
CHEESE.

COOK ON LOW 5-6 HOUR

SERVINGS: 4

The hardest thing about riding a horse, is the ground.
~Anonymous

Egg & Potato Casserole

12 EGGS
3 POTATOES, CHOPPED
1 CUP OF CHIVES, CHOPPED
1 CUP MILK
6 SLICES BACON, COOKED & CHOPPED
1 TEASPOON PEPPER
1/2 TEASPOON SALT

MIX ALL INGREDIENTS. POUR INTO BUTTERED SLOW COOKER.

COOK ON LOW 4-5 HOURS OR UNTIL EGGS ARE COOKED THROUGH.

SERVINGS: 4-6

The wind of heaven is what blows between a horse's ears. ~Arabian proverb

Egg & Broccoli Casserole

24 ounces cottage cheese
6 eggs, beaten
2 cups shredded cheddar or colby jack cheese
3 strips of bacon, cooked and cut into bite sized
pieces or 1/2 cup ham, cubed
1/3 cup flour
1/4 cup butter, melted
1/2 onion, chopped
1/8 teaspoon salt
1 cup mushrooms, sliced
2 cups broccoli, chopped
1 cup walnuts, chopped fine

Set cheese & nuts aside. Mix remaining ingredients.
Pour into greased slow cooker. Add cheese 15
minutes before serving. Top with nuts.

Cook on low 3-4 hours or until eggs are cooked
through.

Servings: 4

Do not spur a free horse. ~Latin proverb

GRAINS & FRUIT

1/4 CUP CRACKED WHEAT
3 TABLESPOONS BARLEY
2 TABLESPOONS CORNMEAL
1/2 CUP OATS
1/4 CUP BROWN RICE
1/2 CUP HONEY
1/4 CUP DRIED CRANBERRIES
1/4 CUP DRIED CHERRIES
1/2 CUP CHOPPED DRIED APRICOTS
1 TABLESPOON CINNAMON
3 CUPS WATER
1 TABLESPOONS VANILLA
1/2 CUP WALNUTS, CHOPPED
1/2 CUP SUNFLOWER SEEDS

COAT THE INSIDE OF THE SLOW COOKER WITH BUTTER.
COMBINE ALL INGREDIENTS, EXCEPT NUTS & SEEDS.

COOK ON LOW 5-6 HOURS, HIGH 3-4 HOURS. TOP WITH
NUTS & SEEDS WHEN SERVING.

SERVINGS: 4

To ride a horse is to ride the sky. ~Author Unknown

Oatmeal

2 CUPS MILK

1/4 CUP BROWN SUGAR

1 TABLESPOON BUTTER, MELTED

1/8 TEASPOON SALT

1/2 CUP RAISINS AND OR CHOPPED DATES

1 TEASPOON CINNAMON

1 CUP STEEL CUT OATS

1 CUP FINELY CHOPPED APPLES

1/4 CUP CHOPPED WALNUTS OR ALMONDS (OPTIONAL)

BUTTER THE SIDES & BOTTOM OF THE SLOW COOKER. MIX ALL INGREDIENTS TOGETHER, EXCEPT NUTS. POUR INTO SLOW COOKER.

COOK ON LOW 3-4 HOURS. TOP WITH NUTS.

SERVINGS: 2

In westerns you were permitted to kiss your horse but never your girl. ~Gary Cooper

PORRIDGE

1/4 CUP CRACKED WHEAT
1 CUP STEEL CUT OATS
3 CUPS WATER
1/4 CUP WHEAT GERM
1 CUP APPLES, CHOPPED
1 TEASPOON CINNAMON

STIR ALL INGREDIENTS TOGETHER IN SLOW COOKER.

COOK ON LOW 6-8 HOURS. TOP WITH MILK, HONEY AND RAISINS.

SERVINGS: 4

It is best not to swap horses while crossing the river.
~Abraham Lincoln

SAUSAGE & EGG CASSEROLE

12 EGGS, BEATEN

12 SLICES OF BREAD

2 1/4 CUPS MILK

2 CUPS GRATED CHEDDAR OR MONTEREY JACK CHEESE

6 SAUSAGE LINKS, CHOPPED INTO BITE SIZED PIECES

2 TEASPOONS GROUND PEPPER

1/2 ONION, CHOPPED

2 TABLESPOONS MUSTARD

1 GREEN PEPPER, DICED

1 PACKAGE MUSHROOMS, SLICED

COAT THE INSIDE OF THE SLOW COOKER WITH BUTTER.
TEAR BREAD INTO BITE SIZED PIECES. PLACE BREAD PIECES
IN THE BOTTOM OF THE SLOW COOKER, THEN LAYER WITH
SOME OF THE CHEESE, ONION & SAUSAGE. CONTINUE TO
LAYER. MIX TOGETHER ALL OTHER INGREDIENTS. POUR
OVER BREAD. TOP WITH MUSHROOMS.

COOK ON LOW 5-6 HOURS OR UNTIL EGGS ARE COOKED
THROUGH.

SERVINGS: 6

Horses are scared of 2 things—things that move, and things that don't. ~Anonymous

SOUTHWEST EGGS

12 EGGS
1 CUP MILK
1 LARGE CAN DICED GREEN CHILIES
1/2 ONION, CHOPPED
1/8 TEASPOON SALT
1 CUP SHREDDED CHEDDAR CHEESE

COAT THE INSIDE OF THE SLOW COOKER WITH COOKING
SPRAY OR BUTTER. MIX ALL INGREDIENTS TOGETHER.
POUR INTO SLOW COOKER.

COOK ON LOW 3-4 HOURS OR UNTIL EGGS ARE COOKED
THROUGH. TOP WITH CHEESE 15 MINUTES BEFORE
SERVING OR COOK UNTIL MELTED.

SERVINGS: 6

A horse loves freedom, and the weariest old workhorse will roll on the ground or break into a lumbering gallop when he is turned loose into the open. ~Gerald Rafferty

Spinach & Eggs Florentine

2 CUPS SHREDDED SHARP CHEDDAR CHEESE

2 CUPS FRESH SPINACH, TORN

6 EGGS

2 SLICES WHITE BREAD, WITHOUT CRUSTS, TORN INTO BITE SIZED PIECES

1/2 CUP GREEN ONIONS, CHOPPED FINE

1 CUP SLICED MUSHROOMS

1 RED PEPPER, CHOPPED

1 CUP MILK

1 TEASPOON PAPRIKA

1/8 TEASPOON SALT

1/4 TEASPOON PEPPER

PLACE A LAYER OF BREAD INTO BOTTOM OF GREASED SLOW COOKER, ADD HALF OF THE CHEESE, SPINACH, MUSHROOMS, ONIONS AND RED PEPPER. CONTINUE LAYERING. MIX TOGETHER EGGS, MILK, SALT & PEPPER. POUR OVER LAYERS. SPRINKLE REMAINING CHEESE & PAPRIKA ON TOP.

COOK ON LOW 3-4 HOURS

SERVINGS: 6

A man that don't love a horse, there is something the matter with him. ~Will Rogers

Turkey & Egg Breakfast

6 EGGS
1 POUND GROUND TURKEY
6 BREAKFAST SAUSAGES OR STRIPS OF BACON, COOKED
& CUT INTO BITE SIZED PIECES
1 TABLESPOON GARLIC, MINCED
1/2 ONION, CHOPPED
3 CARROTS, CHOPPED
1 CUP BLUE CHEESE DRESSING
1 LEMON SQUEEZED
1 TABLESPOON PEPPER
1 PINCH SALT

BUTTER THE SIDES & BOTTOM OF SLOW COOKER. MIX ALL
INGREDIENTS TOGETHER. POUR INTO SLOW COOKER.

COOK ON LOW 4-6 HOURS

SERVINGS: 4-6

Many a shabby foal makes a fine horse. ~Irish proverb

The Iberian Horse

The Iberian horses were bred in the countries of Spain and Portugal on the Iberian peninsula. The origins of the breed date back to 20,000 B.C. They consist of a number of different Spanish breeds. The Lusitano (PSL), the Sorraia, and the Andalusian (PRE) are just three of the seventeen recognized breeds.

These horses were imported with Columbus and Cortes in the late 1400's and early 1500's, when they were shipped across the ocean to the North American continent. The Mustang, American Quarter Horse, Appaloosa, Paint, Tennessee Walking Horse, and American Saddlebred, along with many other breeds of horses, can trace their ancestry to the Iberian Horses.

These elegant equines were used predominantly for war, and as in days gone by, they are still selectively bred for stamina, braveness, tolerance for pain, carefulness, and a willing and eager demeanor. In ancient times of war, their courage allowed them to charge into battle, and the early military maneuvers created the discipline of dressage. They were selectively bred so that the dressage, or military exercises, were easily retained and remembered. Constant demands from the rider were met with tolerance, not annoyance or surly behavior, and when they were not being used for war, their minds and bodies were kept in shape with bullfighting. Through careful breeding, a horse with cow sense was created. This desire and ability to work with cattle was passed on to the modern day Quarter horse.

The Iberian horses are a light framed, yet powerful equine with a swan like neck, clean throatlatch, well angled shoulder, a powerful chest, a high step and large rounded hindquarter. This type of conformation allows these breeds of horses to collect easily and maneuver quickly while moving with elegance and grace. In the past, this made them popular with warriors as well as royalty.

Today they are used all over the world in a variety of different disciplines.

Andalusian Horse

Appetizers

ARTICHOKE CHEESE DIP

3 CUPS CHEDDAR CHEESE
1 CAN CREAM OF MUSHROOM SOUP
2 TEASPOONS WORCESTERSHIRE SAUCE
1/4 CUP EVAPORATED MILK
1 TEASPOON DRY MUSTARD
1/2 CUP CHOPPED ROASTED RED PEPPER
1 CAN ARTICHOKE HEARTS, DRAINED & CHOPPED.

COMBINE ALL INGREDIENTS IN SLOW COOKER. STIR TO MIX.

COOK ON LOW 2-3 HOURS, HIGH NOT RECOMMENDED

Horses and children, I often think, have a lot of the good sense there is in the world. ~Josephine Dermot Robinson

Bacon Cheese Dip

2 PACKAGES CREAM CHEESE, CUT INTO CUBES
4 CUPS SHREDDED SHARP CHEDDAR CHEESE
1 CUP HALF & HALF
2 TABLESPOONS CHOPPED ONION
1/4 TEASPOON CAYENNE PEPPER
2 TABLESPOONS MUSTARD
1 TABLESPOON WORCESTERSHIRE SAUCE
1 POUND BACON, COOKED & DICED

COMBINE ALL INGREDIENTS IN SLOW COOKER.

COOK ON LOW 1-2 HOURS. STIR. SERVE ON TOASTED
BREAD OR CRACKERS.

*A horse never runs so fast as when he has other horses
to catch up and outpace. ~Ovid*

Honeyed Chicken Wings

2 POUNDS CHICKEN WINGS
1/2 TEASPOON PEPPER
1 CUP HONEY
1/4 CUP SOY SAUCE
2 TABLESPOONS KETCHUP
2 GARLIC CLOVES, MINCED
1 TABLESPOON FRESH GINGER, MINCED

PLACE CHICKEN WINGS IN SLOW COOKER. MIX TOGETHER
ALL OTHER INGREDIENTS. POUR OVER CHICKEN.

COOK ON LOW 6-7 HOURS. HIGH NOT RECOMMENDED.

No hour of time is lost that is spent in the saddle.
~Winston Churchill

CHEX SCRAMBLE

2 CUPS WHEAT CHEX
2 CUPS CORN CHEX
2 CUPS RICE CHEX
3 CUPS PRETZEL STICKS
1 CAN SALTED MIXED NUTS
1 TEASPOON GARLIC POWDER
1 TEASPOON CELERY SEED
4 TABLESPOONS GRATED PARMESAN
1/2 CUP MELTED BUTTER

POUR ALL INGREDIENTS INTO GREASED SLOW COOKER.
DRIZZLE MELTED BUTTER OVER THE TOP. MIX TOGETHER.

COOK ON LOW 2-3 HOURS, HIGH NOT RECOMMENDED.
POUR ONTO PAPER TOWEL, LET COOL FOR 1 HOUR BEFORE
SERVING.

A horse is worth more than riches. ~Spanish proverb

CHICKEN NACHOS

2 POUNDS BONELESS SKINLESS CHICKEN
1 PACKAGE OR 3 TABLESPOONS TACO SEASONING MIX
1 CAN PINTO BEANS, DRAINED
2 CANS DICED TOMATOES, DRAINED
1 CAN CHOPPED GREEN CHILIES
3 TABLESPOONS LIME JUICE
1 CAN CHOPPED OLIVES
1 MEDIUM ONION, DICED
1 JALAPENO PEPPER, DICED (OPTIONAL)
2 CUPS SHREDDED CHEESE
TORTILLA-STYLE CHIPS

PLACE ALL INGREDIENTS IN SLOW COOKER, EXCLUDING
TORTILLA CHIPS, 1/4 OF ONION & CHEESE.

COOK ON LOW 3-4 HOURS. PLACE TORTILLA CHIPS ON
SERVING PLATE. TOP WITH SLOW COOKER MIXTURE,
REMAINING ONION & CHEESE.

I know there is money in horses . . I put it there!
~Anonymous

Jack Russell Dogs

3 PACKAGES OF HOT DOGS CUT INTO BITE SIZE PIECES
1 BOTTLE OF BEER
1/4 CUP WHITE WINE
2 TABLESPOONS DRY MUSTARD
1 CUP BROWN SUGAR
1/2 CHOPPED ONION
3 TABLESPOONS WET MUSTARD
1 TABLESPOON WORCESTERSHIRE SAUCE
2 TABLESPOONS BARBEQUE SAUCE
1/4 TEASPOON CAYENNE PEPPER

POUR BEER INTO SLOW COOKER. STIR IN ALL OTHER
INGREDIENTS, PLACING HOT DOGS IN LAST.

COOK ON LOW 3-4 HOURS

Whether you regard the horse with awe or love, it is impossible to escape the sheer power of his presence.
~Mary Wanless

SEAFOOD DIP

2 CANS CREAM OF CELERY SOUP
3 CUPS CHEDDAR CHEESE
1 CUP DICED LOBSTER
1 CUP SHRIMP
1 CUP CRABMEAT
1/4 TEASPOON GROUND PEPPER
1/8 TEASPOON PAPRIKA
1/8 TEASPOON CAYENNE PEPPER
1 TEASPOON GRATED GINGER
1/4 CUP DRY WHITE WINE OR LOW OR NO SODIUM
VEGETABLE BROTH

COMBINE ALL INGREDIENTS IN SLOW COOKER, STIR
TOGETHER.

COOK ON LOW 3-4 HOURS, HIGH NOT RECOMMENDED

*No philosopher so thoroughly comprehends us as dogs
and horses. ~Herman Melville*

SPICED NUTS

2 POUNDS MIX OF PECAN & WALNUT HALVES & WHOLE
ALMONDS
1/2 CUP MELTED BUTTER
1 TABLESPOON CHILI POWDER
1/2 TEASPOON CAYENNE PEPPER
1/4 TEASPOON SALT
1 TEASPOON DRIED BASIL
1 TEASPOON DRIED OREGANO
1 TEASPOON DRIED THYME
1/2 TEASPOON ONION POWDER
1/2 TEASPOON GARLIC POWDER
1/4 TEASPOON DRIED MUSTARD

MELT BUTTER.
COMBINE ALL INGREDIENTS WITH BUTTER.
MIX THOROUGHLY.

COOK ON LOW 2-3 HOURS, HIGH NOT RECOMMENDED.
PLACE ON COOKIE SHEET TO COOL BEFORE SERVING.

A horse gallops with his lungs, perseveres with his heart, and wins with his character. ~Frederico Tesio

SPINACH CHEESE DIP

1 PACKAGE FRESH SPINACH
2 PACKAGES (8 OZ.) CREAM CHEESE, CUBED
1 CUP CHOPPED GREEN ONION
1/2 TEASPOON GARLIC, MINCED
1 TEASPOON GROUND PEPPER
1/4 TEASPOON PAPRIKA
3 CUPS SHREDDED CHEDDAR CHEESE
1 CUP CELERY, CHOPPED FINE
1 CUP CARROTS, CHOPPED FINE
1 CAN WATER CHESTNUTS, DRAINED, CHOPPED
1 CUP WALNUTS, CHOPPED FINE
1/4 CUP DRY WHITE WINE OR LOW OR NO SODIUM
VEGETABLE BROTH

PLACE SPINACH AND GREEN ONIONS, CREAM CHEESE,
GARLIC POWDER, 1.5 CUPS CHEESE, PEPPER, LIQUID AND
PAPRIKA IN SLOW COOKER, MIX TOGETHER.

COOK ON LOW 2-3 HOURS, HIGH NOT RECOMMENDED.
ADD WATER CHESTNUTS, CARROTS, & CELERY, REMAINING
CHEESE & NUTS JUST BEFORE SERVING.

*With horses, something you have never seen before,
happens every day! ~Anonymous*

SWISS FONDUE

2 CLOVES GARLIC, DICED
2 CUPS WHITE WINE OR LOW SODIUM BROTH
1 TABLESPOON LEMON JUICE
3 CUPS SHREDDED SWISS CHEESE
2 CUPS SHREDDED CHEDDAR CHEESE
3 TABLESPOONS FLOUR
3 TABLESPOONS KIRSCH
1/2 TEASPOON BLACK PEPPER
1 TEASPOON GRATED GINGER

1 LOAF OF CRUSTY BREAD, CUT INTO BITE SIZED PIECES
COMBINE ALL INGREDIENTS IN SLOW COOKER, MIX
THOROUGHLY.

COOK ON LOW 2-3 HOURS, HIGH NOT RECOMMENDED

Whenever you observe a horse closely, you feel as if a human being is sitting inside making fun of you.
~Elias Canetti

The Mustang

The first horses to wander the continent that is North America became extinct approximately 10,000 years ago. It is theorized that they were adversely affected by a rapid climate change.

During the Spanish Crusades, many horses that the Conquistadors brought to the new world escaped. They became known as "Mestenos" or stray horses. In later years, many of the horses were purposefully released by the Spaniards to discourage the Native Americans from stealing their better mounts.

The Native Americans quickly assimilated the wild Mustangs into their lives. Transportation, hunting, trading and warring were greatly improved with the introduction of the horse.

During the westward expansion of the 1800s, horses that escaped from traders, trappers, gold miners, settlers and explorers, added their genetics to the already wild herds. By the early 1900's there were more than two million Mustangs. By 1970 fewer than 17,000 still roamed the American west. Most had been killed by ranchers protecting their grazing lands.

In 1971 The Wild Horse and Burro Act created protection for these horses, and today more than 41,000 Mustangs are managed by the Bureau of Land Management in the United States.

Award Winning Photograph,
"Duelling Band Stallions"
by Terry Fitch
of the Wild Horse Freedom Federation

Soups & Stews

Apple & Zucchini Soup

4-6 zucchini, sliced
2 large apples, cored & chopped
1 onion, diced small
1/2 cup rice
4 cups chicken or vegetable stock (low sodium)
2 teaspoons curry powder
1 teaspoon grated ginger
3 tablespoons milk per serving

Pour all ingredients into slow cooker, except milk, stir.

Cook on low 4-5 hours, high 3-4. Puree in blender, add milk and serve.

Servings: 4

The horse through all of its trials has persevered the sweetness of paradise in its blood. ~J. Jensen

Beef & Barley Soup

1 cup soaked & sorted navy beans
1 large onion, chopped fine
3 stalks celery, chopped
4 cloves garlic, diced
3 carrots, chopped
1 cup barley
6 cups low or no sodium beef broth or water
3 pounds stew meat
3 cups fresh torn spinach
1 tablespoon worcestershire sauce

Soak navy beans overnight, drain & sort. Combine all ingredients in slow cooker.

Cook on low 6-8 hours

Servings: 6

The horse is god's gift to man. ~Arab proverb

Beef Stew

1 POUND STEW BEEF
5 CUPS LOW OR NO SODIUM BEEF BROTH OR WATER
2 CLOVES GARLIC, CHOPPED FINE
3 LARGE POTATOES, CHOPPED
1 LARGE ONION, CHOPPED
1 TABLESPOON WORCESTERSHIRE SAUCE
2 TEASPOONS KITCHEN BOUQUET
6 CARROTS, CHOPPED
3 SQUASH, CHOPPED
SALT TO TASTE

COMBINE ALL INGREDIENTS IN SLOW COOKER. FILL WITH
WATER UNTIL 3/4 FULL.

COOK ON LOW 5-6 HOURS, HIGH 3-4 HOURS

SERVINGS: 6

It is the difficult horses that have the most to give.
~Lendon Gray

BBQ Bean Soup

1 POUND NORTHERN BEANS SOAKED OVERNIGHT &
SORTED
1 LARGE ONION, CHOPPED
2 TEASPOONS GROUND PEPPER
3 POUNDS SHORT RIBS
6 CUPS LOW OR NO SODIUM BEEF BROTH OR WATER
1 CUP BARBECUE SAUCE
3 CLOVES GARLIC, FINELY CHOPPED

SET BBQ SAUCE ASIDE. COMBINE ALL INGREDIENTS IN
SLOW COOKER. ADD BBQ SAUCE 1 HOUR BEFORE SERVING.
BEANS SHOULD BE COOKED THROUGH BEFORE ADDING BBQ
SAUCE.

COOK ON LOW 6-8 HOURS

SERVINGS: 6

To me horses and freedom are synonymous. ~Veryl Goodnight

BLACK BEAN SOUP

3 CUPS LOW OR NO SODIUM VEGETABLE BROTH OR WATER
2 ONIONS, CHOPPED
3 CLOVES GARLIC, CHOPPED FINE
1 POUND BLACK BEANS SOAKED, SORTED & DRAINED
1 HAM BONE
2 STALKS CELERY, CHOPPED
1 TEASPOON SALT
2 TEASPOONS GROUND PEPPER OR TO TASTE
3 PIECES COOKED BACON, DICED

COMBINE ALL INGREDIENTS IN SLOW COOKER. FILL SLOW
COOKER 3/4 FULL OF LIQUID. AFTER COOKING REMOVE
HAM BONE. PUREE SOUP.

COOK ON LOW 6-8 HOURS

SERVINGS: 6

*When I bestride him, I soar, I am a hawk: he trots the
air; the earth sings when he touches it; the basest horn
of his hoof is more musical than the pipe of Hermes.
~William Shakespeare*

Broccoli Soup

2 CARROTS, DICED
2 CLOVES GARLIC, CRUSHED
2 STALKS CELERY, CHOPPED
4 CUPS BROCCOLI, CHOPPED
1 CAN CREAM OF CELERY SOUP
3 CUPS LOW OR NO SODIUM CHICKEN BROTH
1 CUP HEAVY WHIPPING CREAM, HALF & HALF. OR MILK
2 CUPS SHREDDED CHEDDAR CHEESE
1 TEASPOON SALT
2 TEASPOONS PEPPER OR TO TASTE

COMBINE ALL INGREDIENTS EXCEPT CREAM, CHEESE &
BUTTER. STIR TOGETHER INTO SLOW COOKER.

COOK ON LOW 6-8 HOURS. ADD CREAM, CHEESE &
BUTTER LAST 30 MINUTES OF COOKING. POUR SOUP INTO
BLENDER AND PUREE. TOP WITH A SPRINKLE OF CHEESE
BEFORE SERVING.

SERVINGS: 6

Good horses make short miles. ~George Herbert

Chicken & Sweet Potato Stew

4 BONELESS CHICKEN BREASTS, CUT INTO SMALL PIECES

4 MEDIUM SWEET POTATOES, CUBED

3 CARROTS, CHOPPED

1 CAN STEWED TOMATOES, DRAINED

1 TEASPOON PAPRIKA

1 TEASPOON BLACK PEPPER

1/4 TEASPOON NUTMEG

1/4 TEASPOON GROUND CINNAMON

1 TEASPOON CELERY SEED

1/4 TEASPOON SALT

1/4 TEASPOON GROUND GINGER

5 CUPS LOW OR NO SODIUM CHICKEN BROTH

1 CUP FRESH BASIL, CHOPPED

2 TABLESPOONS ROSEMARY, DICED

COMBINE ALL INGREDIENTS IN SLOW COOKER, STIR.

COOK ON LOW 5-6 HOURS

SERVINGS: 6

A horse a horse! My kingdom for a horse. ~William Shakespeare

CREAMY CHILI

1 POUND GROUND BEEF
1 POUND BEEF TIPS
1 CAN BLACK BEANS, DRAINED
1 CAN RED KIDNEY BEANS, DRAINED
2 CANS CHILI BEANS, UNDRAINED
1 JAR SALSA
2 TOMATOES, CHOPPED
1 BELL PEPPER, CHOPPED
1 ONION, CHOPPED FINE
1 CLOVE GARLIC, MINCED
3 CUPS LOW OR NO SODIUM BEEF BROTH
2 TABLESPOONS CHILI POWDER

COMBINE ALL INGREDIENTS. MIX THOROUGHLY.

COOK ON LOW 3-4 HOURS. TOP WITH CHEESE AND SOUR CREAM.

SERVINGS: 6

Four things greater than all things are, . . . women and horses and power and war. ~R. Kipling

Corn & Beef Stew

2 POUNDS GROUND BEEF
2 GREEN OR RED PEPPERS, DICED
1/2 ONION, DICED
6 RED POTATOES, DICED
2 CARROTS, DICED
1 STALK CELERY, DICED
2 TABLESPOONS BUTTER, MELTED
1 CAN CORN
1 CAN CREAMED CORN
1 PACKAGE GRAVY MIX
3 CUPS LOW OR NO SODIUM BEEF BROTH OR WATER
SALT TO TASTE

COMBINE ALL INGREDIENTS IN SLOW COOKER. MIX
THOROUGHLY.

COOK ON LOW 5-6 HOURS

SERVINGS: 4

Dog lovers hate to clean kennels. Horse lovers like cleaning stables. ~M. Dickens

CHICKEN & RICE SOUP

2 POUNDS BONELESS CHICKEN, MINCED
5 CUPS LOW OR NO SODIUM CHICKEN BROTH OR WATER
1 CAN CREAM OF CHICKEN SOUP
3 STALKS CELERY, CHOPPED
1 SMALL ONION, DICED
3 CARROTS, CHOPPED
2 CUPS SPINACH, TORN INTO SMALL PIECES
1/2 CUP UNCOOKED WHITE RICE

COMBINE ALL INGREDIENTS IN SLOW COOKER. STIR TO MIX.

COOK ON LOW 3-5 HOURS

SERVINGS: 4

I can always tell which is the front end of the horse, but beyond that, my art is not above the ordinary. ~Mark Twain

Italian Sausage Stew

1 POUND GROUND BEEF
1 POUND ITALIAN SAUSAGE, CUT INTO SMALL PIECES
3/4 CUP DRIED BREAD CRUMBS
1 CUP GRATED PARMESAN CHEESE
1/4 CUP MILK
1 EGG
1 TEASPOON DRIED BASIL
2 CLOVES GARLIC, MINCED
1/2 TEASPOON SALT
1 TEASPOON BLACK PEPPER
1 TEASPOON ROSEMARY, CRUSHED
4 CUPS LOW OR NO SODIUM BEEF BROTH OR WATER
2 TABLESPOONS TOMATO PASTE
1/2 TEASPOON CRUSHED RED PEPPER FLAKES
1 BAG SPINACH, TORN
2 CUPS COOKED NOODLES

TO MAKE MEATBALLS COMBINE: MEAT, BREAD CRUMBS, EGG, AND MILK. PLACE IN SLOW COOKER. COMBINE ALL OTHER INGREDIENTS, EXCEPT SPINACH AND NOODLES. POUR OVER MEATBALLS.

COOK ON LOW 4-5 HOURS. ADD SPINACH & HOT NOODLES JUST BEFORE SERVING. TOP WITH PARMESAN CHEESE.

⊌

That hoss wasn't built to tread the earth, he took natural to the air, and every time he went aloft, he tried to leave me there. ~Anonymous

MEDITERRANEAN STEW

2 CUPS LOW OR NO SODIUM VEGETABLE BROTH OR WATER

1 BUTTERNUT SQUASH, CUBED AND PEELED

2 CUPS EGGPLANT, CUBED

2 CUPS ZUCCHINI, CUBED

2 CUPS FROZEN PEAS, THAWED

1 LARGE CAN DICED TOMATOES, UNDRAINED

1 MEDIUM ONION, CHOPPED

2 CARROTS, SLICED

1/2 CUP RAISINS

1 TEASPOON GROUND CUMIN

1/2 TEASPOON GROUND TURMERIC

1/2 TEASPOON CRUSHED RED PEPPER

1/2 TEASPOON PAPRIKA

1 CLOVE GARLIC, MINCED

SALT TO TASTE

PLACE ALL INGREDIENTS IN SLOW COOKER, STIR.

COOK ON LOW 4-6 HOURS.

SERVINGS: 4-6

Feeling down? Saddle up. ~Author Unknown

NACHO CHEESE SOUP

1 POUND BONELESS CHICKEN, CUT INTO PIECES
2 LARGE CANS MEXICAN STYLE STEWED TOMATOES,
UNDRAINED
1 CAN CORN, DRAINED
1 LARGE CAN NACHO CHEESE SOUP
2 CUPS SHREDDED CHEESE
1 JALAPENO, DICED

SET CHEESE ASIDE. POUR ALL OTHER INGREDIENTS INTO
SLOW COOKER.

COOK ON LOW 3-4 HOURS, HIGH NOT RECOMMENDED
SPRINKLE WITH CHEESE BEFORE SERVING.

SERVINGS: 6

When I can't ride anymore, I shall still keep horses as long as I can hobble about with a bucket and a wheelbarrow. When I can't hobble, I shall roll my wheelchair out to the fence of the field where my horses graze and watch them. ~Monica Dickens

Potato Soup

6 POTATOES, CUT INTO CUBES
2 ONIONS, DICED
3 CARROTS, DICED
3 STALKS CELERY, DICED
3 CUPS LOW OR NO SODIUM CHICKEN BROTH
1 TABLESPOON BASIL, DICED
1/4 TEASPOON SALT OR TO TASTE
1 TEASPOON PEPPER
1/4 CUP FLOUR
3 PIECES COOKED BACON, CRUMBLED
2 CUPS HALF & HALF OR MILK

STIR TOGETHER MILK WITH FLOUR, SET ASIDE. MIX ALL
OTHER INGREDIENTS.

COOK ON LOW 3-4 HOURS, HIGH 2-3 HOURS. ADD MILK
& FLOUR MIXTURE 1 HOUR BEFORE SERVING; TURN TO
LOW.

SERVINGS: 6

He has galloped through young girls dreams, added richness to women's lives, and served men in war and strife. ~Toni Robinson

Pumpkin Soup

1/2 CUP BUTTER, MELTED
2 POUNDS PUMPKIN PEELED AND CUT INTO 1 INCH
SQUARE PIECES
1 MEDIUM ONION, CHOPPED
2 CLOVES GARLIC, MINCED
2 TEASPOONS BROWN SUGAR
3 CUPS LOW SODIUM VEGETABLE STOCK OR WATER
1 CUP MILK
PINCH OF CLOVES
SPRINKLE OF NUTMEG
1/4 CUP CILANTRO, MINCED
1/4 CUP PUMPKIN SEEDS, CHOPPED

STIR TOGETHER ALL INGREDIENTS IN SLOW COOKER,
EXCEPT NUTMEG, CILANTRO, & PUMPKIN SEEDS.

COOK ON LOW 8-10 HOURS.

PUREE IN BLENDER AND GARNISH WITH NUTMEG, CILANTRO
& PUMPKIN SEEDS.

SERVINGS: 4

Boot, saddle, to horse, and away! ~R. Browning

Tortilla Soup

1 POUND BONELESS CHICKEN, CUBED

1 CAN DICED TOMATOES, UNDRAINED

1 CAN GREEN CHILI PEPPERS, DICED

2 CANS KIDNEY BEANS, DRAINED

1 PACKAGE OR 2 TABLESPOONS TACO SEASONING

1 CAN CORN, UNDRAINED

1 ONION, CHOPPED

1 LARGE CAN ENCHILADA SAUCE

MIX ALL INGREDIENTS TOGETHER.

COOK ON LOW 8-10 HOURS, HIGH 4-6 HOURS.

TOP WITH CHEESE & SOUR CREAM

SERVINGS: 4-6

A good man will take care of his horses and dogs, not only while they are young, but also when they are old and past service. ~Plutarch

The Appaloosa

Through trading and thievery the plains Indians acquired horses from the Pueblo Indians after they revolted against the Spanish. By the beginning of the 1700s the Nez Perce tribe of Washington and Idaho had become adept at breeding spotted horses for stamina, bravery, and overall athletic superiority. The Appaloosa acquired its name from the Palouse River Valley where the horses were bred and raised. It is a region in which the Snake River and the Palouse River flow together and where the main village of the Native American tribe was established. This breed of horse was known amongst the settlers as a Palouse horse, and later the words merged into Appaloosey and then Appaloosa. They were highly prized for their beautiful spotted coat pattern, as well as their superior hardiness, and stamina.

The Nez Perce became exceptional horseman; they were the first Native American tribe to practice selective breeding. The mediocre stallions were gelded and the substandard mares traded. They became a wealthy tribe, with top-quality stock numbering into the thousands.

In 1860 a treaty with the Nez Perce was broken when gold was discovered on seven million acres of tribal land that had been given to them by the United States government. Almost instantly settlers rushed in and began the town of Lewiston, Idaho. A vastly reduced reservation was then established in 1863; however, not all of the Nez Perce would sign the treaty. Those that chose to be farmers concurred while many of the horsemen of the Palouse River Valley did not. Conflicts began to break out between the settlers and the nontreaty Indians. Eventually a battle erupted in White Bird Canyon on June 17, 1877. This became known as the Nez Perce War of 1877. The unsigned Indians fled with 3,000 horses while being chased by the cavalry as they headed to Canada. The trek included women, children and the elderly. The renegades eluded the cavalry for three and a half months, traveling 1,300 miles on their superior Appaloosa horses. The surrender took place just 42 miles from the safety of the Canadian border on October 7, 1877. Although promises had been made that the last surviving spotted horses of the Chief Joseph band would be relinquished back to the tribe upon its surrender, the promise, like so many others, was broken.

One little known fact is that in 1994, one hundred and seventeen years after the Nez Perce were ordered by General Howard to move onto the reservation, an old herd of Appaloosas was gifted back to a direct descendant of Chief Ollokot, Irvin Waters. Chief Ollokot was Chief Joseph's brother. His people did not have enough time to gather the thousands of horses that were spread over a million acres, before arriving at the reservation, therefore, Chief Ollokot entrusted these horses to a rancher that he respected and who had become his friend. The rancher and his children's children honored their pledge; they kept the "Old herd" of appaloosas until 1994, when they returned them to Mr. Waters.

The Appaloosa Horse Club was established in America in 1938 to promote this special breed of horse. Today the Appaloosa Horse Club is the third largest breed registry in the world.

Nez Perce family with Appaloosas
in North Central Idaho.
Photo courtesy of The Clearwater
Historical Museum.

Beef

ASTONISHING BEEF

1 POT ROAST
8 PEPPERONCINIS, DICED
3 TO 4 CLOVES GARLIC, CHOPPED
1 ONION, CHOPPED
1/2 TEASPOON BLACK PEPPER
1/2 CUP ITALIAN SALAD DRESSING
2 TABLESPOONS STEAK SAUCE

PUT ROAST IN SLOW COOKER. MIX ALL OTHER INGREDIENTS TOGETHER. POUR OVER ROAST.

COOK ON LOW 8-10 HOURS, HIGH 4-6 HOURS.

TO THICKEN JUICES MAKE A ROUX WITH 2 TABLESPOONS BUTTER AND 1 TABLESPOON FLOUR OR 1 TABLESPOON CORNSTARCH ADDED TO LIQUID. ADD 1 HOUR BEFORE SERVING.

SERVINGS: 4

The hooves of horses! Oh! Witching and sweet is the music earth steals from the iron-shod feet; no whisper of a lover, no trilling of a bird, can stir me as much as the hooves of the horses have stirred. ~Will H. Ogilvie

Beef Stroganoff

1 POUND STEAK, CUBED OR GROUND BEEF
3 CLOVES GARLIC, CHOPPED FINE
1 ONION, CHOPPED FINE
1/8 CUP DRY WHITE WINE
1 CAN CREAM OF MUSHROOM SOUP
1 TO 2 CUPS SOUR CREAM OR PLAIN YOGURT
1/2 TEASPOON CRUSHED RED PEPPER
1 TEASPOON GROUND PEPPER
1 PACKAGE MUSHROOMS, SLICED
1 TABLESPOON CORNSTARCH OR FLOUR FOR THICKENING

PLACE BEEF IN SLOW COOKER. MIX TOGETHER ALL OTHER
INGREDIENTS EXCEPT SOUP, MUSHROOMS AND SOUR
CREAM. POUR OVER BEEF.

COOK ON LOW 8-10 HOURS, HIGH 5-6 HOURS. MAKE A
CORNSTARCH MIXTURE OR ROUX TO THICKEN SAUCE. MIX
IN SLOW COOKER ALONG WITH SOUP, MUSHROOMS AND
SOUR CREAM OR YOGHURT 1 HOUR BEFORE SERVING.
SERVE ON NOODLES OR RICE.

SERVINGS: 4-6

O for a horse with wings! ~William Shakespeare

CALIENTE MEATLOAF

2 POUNDS LEAN GROUND BEEF
1 ONION, CHOPPED
1 CUP SEASONED BREADCRUMBS
1/2 CUP BELL PEPPER, CHOPPED
1/4 CUP CHILI SAUCE
1/8 CUP MILK
5 CLOVES GARLIC, MINCED
2 EGGS, LIGHTLY BEATEN
2 TABLESPOONS SPICY MUSTARD
1/2 TEASPOON SALT
1/2 TEASPOON OREGANO
1 TEASPOON DRIED BASIL
1/4 TEASPOON BLACK PEPPER
1/8 TEASPOON DRY MUSTARD

IN SLOW COOKER MIX TOGETHER ALL OF THE INGREDIENTS EXCEPT 1/8 CUP CHILI SAUCE.

COOK ON LOW 5-6 HOURS, HIGH 3-4 HOURS. TOP WITH CHILI SAUCE.

SERVINGS: 3-4

A fly may sting a stately horse and make him wince; but one is but an insect, and the other a horse still.
~Samuel Johnson

COFFEE ROAST

1 CHUCK ROAST
2 CLOVES GARLIC, QUARTERED
1/2 CUP BLACK COFFEE
1/2 CUP LOW OR NO SODIUM BEEF BROTH
1 TABLESPOONS LOW SODIUM SOY SAUCE
1 TABLESPOON WORCHESTERSHIRE SAUCE
SALT AND PEPPER TO TASTE
3-4 POTATOES, HALVED

CREATE SMALL SLITS THROUGHOUT THE ROAST. PUSH SLIVERS OF GARLIC INTO SLITS. PLACE ROAST IN SLOW COOKER. MIX COFFEE AND OTHER INGREDIENTS. POUR OVER ROAST. PLACE POTATOES ALONG SIDE OF ROAST.

COOK ON LOW 6-8 HOURS, HIGH 5-6 HOURS. CREATE CORNSTARCH MIXTURE TO THICKEN JUICES.

SERVINGS: 4-6

Through his mane and tail the high wind sings,
fanning the hairs, who wave the feather'd wings.
~William Shakespeare

ITALIAN POT ROAST

1 ROAST
1 PACKAGE POT ROAST SEASONINGS
1/2 CUP ITALIAN DRESSING
3 TABLESPOONS DRY WHITE WINE
3 CARROTS, CHOPPED
1 ONION, CHOPPED
4 STALKS CELERY, CHOPPED
1 PINCH CRUSHED RED PEPPER

PLACE ROAST IN SLOW COOKER. COMBINE LIQUIDS AND
SEASONINGS, MIX THOROUGHLY. POUR OVER ROAST. TOP
WITH VEGETABLES.

COOK ON LOW 8-10 HOURS, HIGH 4-6 HOURS

SERVINGS: 4-6

*Horses have hooves to carry them over frost and snow;
hair, to protect them from wind and cold, they eat grass
and drink water, and fling up their heels . . . such is
the real nature of horses. ~Chang Ttzu*

LASAGNA

1 POUND GROUND BEEF
1 CAN TOMATO PASTE
1 JAR SPAGHETTI SAUCE
1/8 TEASPOON SALT
1 TEASPOON DRIED OREGANO
3 TABLESPOONS FRESH BASIL, TORN
1 RED OR GREEN PEPPER, CHOPPED FINE
2 CARROTS, CHOPPED
1 PACKAGE NO-COOK LASAGNA NOODLES
4 CUPS SHREDDED MOZZARELLA CHEESE
2 CUPS RICOTTA CHEESE
2 CUPS GRATED PARMESAN CHEESE

MIX BEEF, RICOTTA, SPICES, PEPPER, CARROTS &
SALT. MIX SPAGHETTI SAUCE AND TOMATO PASTE IN A
SEPARATE BOWL. POUR A SMALL AMOUNT OF SAUCE IN
SLOW COOKER. ADD A LAYER OF NOODLES, THEN MEAT
MIXTURE, AND CHEESES. CONTINUE LAYERING. TOP WITH
MOZZARELLA AND PARMESAN CHEESES.

COOK ON LOW 5-6 HOURS, HIGH 3-4

SERVINGS: 6

They say that princes learn no art truly, but the art of horsemanship. The reason is, the brave beast is no flatterer. He will throw a prince as soon as his groom.
~Ben Johnson

MUSTARD POT ROAST

2 POUND CHUCK ROAST
4 TABLESPOONS WORCESTERSHIRE SAUCE
2 TABLESPOONS DIJON OR HORSERADISH MUSTARD
1/2 ONION, FINELY CHOPPED
1 TEASPOON GARLIC, CHOPPED FINE
4 POTATOES, SCRUBBED

POUR MUSTARD, ONION, GARLIC & WORCESTERSHIRE
SAUCE IN SLOW COOKER, STIR. PLACE ROAST IN LIQUID.
PUT POTATOES ALONG THE SIDE.

COOK ON LOW 6-8 HOURS, HIGH NOT RECOMMENDED

ADD 2 TABLESPOONS CORNSTARCH OR MAKE A ROUX WITH
1 TABLESPOONS BUTTER AND 2 TABLESPOONS FLOUR.
ADD 1 HOUR BEFORE SERVING TO THICKEN SAUCE.

SERVINGS: 4-6

They're the most forgiving creatures that god ever made. ~Nicholas Evans

Peppers & Steak

1 ROUND STEAK, CUT INTO STRIPS
1/2 CUP FLOUR
1 ONION, QUARTERED
3 GREEN PEPPERS, CUT INTO STRIPS
4 CARROTS, SLICED
1 LARGE CAN DICED TOMATOES, DRAINED
1 PACKAGE MUSHROOMS, SLICED
2 CLOVES GARLIC, CHOPPED FINE
1 TEASPOON BLACK PEPPER
1/4 TEASPOON SALT
2 TABLESPOONS STEAK SAUCE

SET FLOUR & MEAT ASIDE. MIX ALL INGREDIENTS, POUR INTO SLOW COOKER. COAT MEAT IN FLOUR. PLACE MEAT IN SLOW COOKER.

COOK ON LOW 6-8 HOURS

SERVINGS: 4-6

Riding a horse is not a gentle hobby, to be picked up and laid down like a game of solitaire, it is a grand passion. ~Ralph Waldo Emerson

Summer Steak

1.5 POUND ROUND STEAK, CUT INTO BITE SIZE PIECES
1/8 CUP FLOUR
1/4 TEASPOON LEMON JUICE
1 ONION, CHOPPED
6 TOMATOES, CHOPPED
1 PACKAGE MUSHROOMS, SLICED
4 TABLESPOONS MOLASSES
3 TABLESPOONS SOY SAUCE
1 TEASPOON GRATED GINGER
3 ASPARAGUS CHOPPED INTO BITE SIZE PIECES
1/4 CUP LOW OR NO SODIUM BROTH OR DRY RED WINE

PLACE STEAK IN BAG WITH FLOUR. SHAKE BAG TO COAT.
MIX TOGETHER ALL OTHER INGREDIENTS IN SLOW COOKER,
EXCEPT ASPARAGUS & MUSHROOMS. ADD STEAK. COOK
ON LOW 5-6 HOURS. ADD ASPARAGUS & MUSHROOMS
THE LAST 30 MINUTES OF COOKING.

SERVE ON RICE OR NOODLES

SERVINGS: 4

In riding a horse, we borrow freedom. ~Helen Thompson

Stuffed Peppers

1 POUND HAMBURGER
1 CUP PRE-COOKED RICE
1/4 CUP BLUE CHEESE CRUMBLES
1/8 CUP FRESH ROSEMARY, MINCED
1/8 CUP FRESH BASIL, CHOPPED FINE
2 CLOVES GARLIC, MINCED
PINCH SALT
PINCH GROUND BLACK PEPPER
1/2 CUP PESTO
4-6 PEPPERS, SEEDED
4 TABLESPOONS WATER

POUR WATER INTO SLOW COOKER. REMOVE THE SEEDS
FROM PEPPERS. KEEPING PEPPERS TO ONE SIDE, MIX ALL
INGREDIENTS TOGETHER, STUFF PEPPERS.

COOK ON LOW 4-6 HOURS, HIGH 3-4 HOURS.

SERVINGS: 4-6

Horses if god made anything more beautiful, he kept it to himself. ~Anonymous

The Thoroughbred

The Thoroughbred breed of horse was developed in England in the 17th and 18th centuries. Throughout history they have been used predominantly for the popular sport of horse racing. Racing on the flat was recorded in history as early as 1174, when four mile races were held in London. Horse racing gained popularity and continued through the middle ages and into today. Native horses of England were crossed with Barb, Arabian and Turkoman bloodlines, which created hot blooded, swift, agile, bold, and spirited steeds.

The first Thoroughbreds were imported to America in 1730 where match races were held in the streets of many towns and cities. The Jockey Club of America was formed in 1894 in New York.

This breed of horse has been very influential in the development of many other breeds. The Appaloosa, Quarter Horse, Standardbred, Anglo-Arabian, Morgan, Paint and a vast number of Warmblood breeds are infused with blood of the Thoroughbred.

Today the Thoroughbred's long lean body and excellent stamina are in demand for many riding disciplines: racing, show jumping, eventing, polo, dressage, barrel racing and fox hunting are just some of sports in which the Thoroughbred excels.

Cook 431 Man o' War on track with Andy Schuttinger up, Travers Stakes @ Saratoga, 8/21/1920

Thoroughbred, Man O' War
Photograph Courtesy Of:
Keeneland Library

Lamb

APRICOT LAMB IN CURRY

6 LAMB CHOPS
1/4 CUP DRY WHITE WINE
3 TEASPOONS CRUSHED GARLIC
2 TABLESPOON CURRY POWDER
1/2 CUP APRICOT JAM
1/2 TABLESPOON MIXED HERBS
1/2 TEASPOON SALT

PLACE LAMB IN SLOW COOKER. COMBINE ALL OTHER
INGREDIENTS. POUR OVER LAMB.

COOK ON LOW 6-8 HOURS, HIGH NOT RECOMMENDED

SERVINGS: 6

And God took a handful of southerly wind, blew his breath upon it, and created the horse. ~Bedouin legend

CURRIED LAMB

1 POUND BONELESS LAMB, CUT INTO BITE SIZED PIECES
1 APPLE, FINELY CHOPPED
1/2 CUP LOW OR NO SODIUM CHICKEN BROTH
1 TABLESPOON CURRY POWDER
1 TEASPOON ROSEMARY, CRUSHED

COMBINE ALL INGREDIENTS IN SLOW COOKER.

COOK ON LOW 6-8 HOURS, HIGH 3-4 HOURS

ADD CORNSTARCH IF NEEDED TO THICKEN SAUCE.
SERVE ON COOKED RICE

SERVINGS: 2-3

If you act like you've only got fifteen minutes, it'll take all day. Act like you've got all day and it'll take fifteen minutes. ~Monty Roberts

Dijon Wine & Lamb

6 LAMB SHANKS
1/2 CUP DRY RED WINE OR LOW OR NO SODIUM BROTH
3 TABLESPOONS DIJON MUSTARD
1 CLOVE GARLIC, MINCED
1 ONION, CHOPPED FINE
1 TABLESPOON LEMON JUICE
3 TABLESPOONS ROSEMARY, CHOPPED FINE
1/2 TEASPOON SALT
1 TEASPOON GROUND PEPPER

SET ASIDE LAMB SHANKS. COMBINE ALL OTHER INGREDIENTS IN SLOW COOKER. MIX THOROUGHLY, ADD LAMB.

COOK ON LOW 6-8 HOURS, HIGH 4-5 HOURS

SERVINGS: 6

There is something about riding down the street on a prancing horse that makes you feel like something, even when you ain't a thing. ~Will Rogers

Korean Lamb

2 POUNDS LAMB
2 TABLESPOONS SOY SAUCE
1 TABLESPOON HONEY
1 TABLESPOON RICE VINEGAR
2 TABLESPOONS SHERRY
2 CLOVES GARLIC, CRUSHED
1 TABLESPOON GRATED GINGER
1/2 CUP CHICKEN STOCK (LOW SODIUM)
1 CAN WATER CHESTNUTS, DICED
1/2 CUP CASHEWS, CHOPPED FINE

PLACE LAMB IN SLOW COOKER. MIX ALL INGREDIENTS EXCEPT WATER CHESTNUTS & CASHEWS. POUR LIQUID & SPICES OVER MEAT.

COOK ON LOW 8-10 HOURS, HIGH 4-6. 30 MINUTES BEFORE SERVING ADD WATER CHESTNUTS & CREATE CORNSTARCH MIXTURE, ADD TO SLOW COOKER TO THICKEN JUICES. SPOON OVER MEAT WHEN SERVED. TOP WITH CASHEWS.

SERVINGS: 4-6

Honor lies in the mane of a horse. ~Herman Melville

LAMB WITH BLUE CHEESE STUFFING

1 PIECE DE-BONED ROASTING LAMB, BUTTERFLIED
3 TABLESPOONS OLIVE OIL
3 TABLESPOONS LEMON JUICE
1/4 CUP GRATED LEMON RIND
1 CLOVE GARLIC, CHOPPED FINE
1 ONION, CHOPPED FINE
1 CUP BREADCRUMBS
1/4 CONTAINER BLUE CHEESE CRUMBLES
1/2 CUP PINE NUTS
1 TABLESPOON MELTED BUTTER
2 TEASPOONS OREGANO, CHOPPED FINE
2 TEASPOONS ROSEMARY, CRUSHED

POUR OLIVE OIL INTO SLOW COOKER. COMBINE BREADCRUMBS, GARLIC, ONION, BUTTER, BLUE CHEESE & PINE NUTS. SPREAD ON LAMB, ROLL & TIE WITH TWINE. IN SEPARATE BOWL MIX OIL, OREGANO, ROSEMARY LEMON RIND & JUICE. RUB LAMB.

COOK ON LOW 8-10 HOURS

SERVINGS: 4

Gypsy gold does not chink and glitter. It gleams in the sun and neighs in the dark. ~Saying of the Gladdagh Gypsies of Galway

LEG OF LAMB

1 LEG OF LAMB
6 CLOVES GARLIC
4 TABLESPOONS FRESH ROSEMARY, CHOPPED FINE
2 TEASPOONS PEPPER
3 TABLESPOONS OLIVE OIL
1/4 CUP SOY SAUCE (REDUCED SODIUM)

CUT SMALL SLITS INTO LAMB. PUSH PIECES OF GARLIC
INTO SLITS. COMBINE ROSEMARY, OIL, SALT & PEPPER.
RUB OVER LEG OF LAMB. POUR SOY SAUCE INTO SLOW
COOKER. PLACE LAMB INSIDE.

COOK ON LOW 8-10 HOURS, HIGH 3-4 HOURS

SERVE ON RICE

SERVINGS: 4

*A pony is a childhood dream, a horse is an adulthood
treasure. ~Rebecca Carrol*

Minted Lamb

1 ROASTING LAMB
3 TABLESPOONS BUTTER, MELTED
3 TABLESPOONS ROSEMARY, CHOPPED FINE
3 TABLESPOONS MINT, MINCED
1/2 TEASPOON SALT
1 TEASPOON PEPPER
1 TABLESPOON GARLIC, MINCED
3 TABLESPOONS LEMON JUICE
2 TABLESPOONS DRY RED WINE
4-6 RED POTATOES
2 CARROTS, CHOPPED THIN

SET LAMB ASIDE. MIX TOGETHER ALL OTHER INGREDIENTS. RUB ON LAMB, POUR REMAINING LIQUID IN SLOW COOKER. PLACE LAMB INSIDE, SURROUND WITH POTATOES. ADD CARROTS LAST 30 MINUTES OF COOKING.

COOK ON LOW 8-10 HOURS, HIGH 4-6 HOURS

SERVINGS: 3-4

Trust in God, but tie your horse. ~Anonymous

PLUM LAMB ROAST

1 PIECE ROASTING LAMB
1 CUP PLUM JAM
1 CUP PLUMS, CHOPPED FINE
1 CUP MUSHROOMS, SLICED
1/4 CUP DRY RED WINE OR LOW OR NO SODIUM BROTH
2 TEASPOONS GRATED GINGER
1 TEASPOON CHILI SAUCE
1 TABLESPOON SOY SAUCE
1 TEASPOON CORN STARCH

PLACE LAMB IN SLOW COOKER. MIX TOGETHER ALL OTHER INGREDIENTS. POUR OVER LAMB. TO THICKEN SAUCE: 1 HOUR BEFORE SERVING, MIX A SMALL AMOUNT OF LIQUID WITH CORNSTARCH. POUR BACK INTO SLOW COOKER. ADD MUSHROOMS.

COOK ON LOW 5-6 HOURS

SERVE ON RICE

SERVINGS: 3-4

Speak your mind, but ride a fast horse. ~Anonymous

Wine & Gingered Lamb

2 POUNDS LAMB STEW MEAT
2 ONIONS, CHOPPED
6 CLOVES GARLIC, CHOPPED
2 TEASPOONS CUMIN
1 TEASPOON GROUND CORIANDER
1 LARGE PIECE GINGER, GRATED
1 CAN BLACK OLIVES, CHOPPED
2 TABLESPOONS CAPERS
1/3 CUP DRY RED WINE

COMBINE ALL INGREDIENTS IN SLOW COOKER. ADD OLIVES
LAST 30 MINUTES OF COOKING. CREATE CORNSTARCH
MIXTURE TO THICKEN SAUCE.

COOK ON LOW 6-8 HOURS, HIGH 3-4 HOURS

SERVE ON RICE.

*Old minds are like old horses; you must exercise them if
you wish to keep them in working order. ~John Adams*

ZINFANDEL LAMB

3 POUNDS LAMB MEAT, CUT INTO BITE SIZED PIECES
1/2 CUP RED ZINFANDEL WINE OR LOW OR NO SODIUM
BROTH
1 TABLESPOON ROSEMARY, CRUSHED
3/4 TEASPOON GROUND CUMIN
1.5 TEASPOONS GROUND CINNAMON
1/4 TEASPOON CRUSHED RED PEPPER
1/2 TEASPOON GROUND CLOVES
3/4 TEASPOON GROUND CARDAMOM
1/4 TEASPOON SAFFRON
1 TABLESPOON GARLIC, MINCED
1 TEASPOON CORIANDER
1 ONION, CHOPPED FINE
3 TOMATOES, CHOPPED
6 CARROTS, SLICED
2 TABLESPOONS GRATED GINGER
1 TABLESPOON SUN-DRIED TOMATO PASTE
1 TABLESPOON LEMON ZEST
2 TABLESPOON HONEY

COMBINE ALL INGREDIENTS IN SLOW COOKER.

COOK ON LOW 6-8 HOURS, HIGH 3-4. TO THICKEN
JUICES: CREATE CORNSTARCH MIXTURE, ADD 1 HOUR
BEFORE SERVING.

SERVINGS: 4-6

I heard a neigh, Oh, such a brisk and melodious neigh it was. My very heart leaped with the sound.
~Nathaniel Hawthorne

The Arabian

Arabians are a breed of horse that evolved on the Arabian peninsula. They are one of the oldest breeds in the world with evidence of their existence dating back 4,500 years. Almost every breed of horse in the world has the blood of the Arabian horse in their genes.

These horses were often brought into the tents of the Bedouins in order to keep them safe from the elements and thieves, thus creating a horse that is a very willing and intelligent companion. The Arabians evolved in the desert, therefore, they have great endurance and are athletically suited for speed in harsh climates. Because they lived in this barren region of open terrain, without protection from predators, they are highly sensitive, alert and swift in movement.

This breed of horse is versatile, and consequently, they are used in many different disciplines. They dominate the world of endurance racing.

Arabian horses have big liquid brown eyes, large nostrils, petite muzzles and distinctive concave or "dished" profiles. They exhibit a long neck with a clean throat latch, and a flat croup with a tail that is set high, giving them an elegant appearance. Many Arabians have 5 lumbar vertebrae instead of the usual 6, and 17 ribs instead of the normal 18.

Napoleon, Alexander the Great, and George Washington are some of the famous people who owned and rode Arabians.

A horse introduced by Nathaniel Harrison was one of the first Arabians to be imported to America in 1725.

Breeding farms were established throughout Europe and America in the 1800s, when many world travelers became infatuated with the breed.

The Arabian Horse Association of America was founded in 1908. It has registered over one million horses to date.

The Emperor of Syria and Arabia had banned the exportation of its prize horses. Only the intervention of president Theodore Roosevelt had enabled Davenport to secure a permit to bring the largest importation of pure desert-bred horses to America, and to change the history of Arabian horses in the U.S. forever. Photo is: "Sheikh Hachem Bey riding his best mare trying out Homer's cowboy saddle which he didn't like." Sheikh of all Anezeh Sheikhs became a close friend of Davenport and assisted him in finding horses to export to the states.

Photo courtesy of the International Museum of the Horse, Kentucky Horse Park

Pork

APRICOT PORK

3 POUNDS PORK
3 BACON STRIPS, COOKED & CRUMBLED
1 CUP APPLES, CHOPPED
1 CUP DRIED APRICOTS, DICED
1 ONION, CHOPPED FINE
4 STALKS CELERY, DICED
1/8 CUP DRY WHITE WINE
1/4 CUP APPLE JUICE
1/4 CUP HONEY
1/8 TEASPOON SALT
1 TEASPOON BLACK PEPPER
1 TABLESPOON GRATED GINGER

PUT PORK IN SLOW COOKER, MIX OTHER INGREDIENTS.
POUR OVER MEAT.

COOK ON LOW 8-10 HOURS. 1 HOUR BEFORE SERVING,
CREATE A CORNSTARCH MIXTURE TO THICKEN JUICES.

SERVINGS: 4-6

A good horse makes short miles. ~George Elliot

Asian Pork

1 PORK ROAST
1/4 CUP SOY SAUCE
1/4 CUP ORANGE MARMALADE
1 TABLESPOON KETCHUP
1 GARLIC CLOVE, CRUSHED
1/2 TEASPOON GRATED GINGER
1/8 TEASPOON CHILI SAUCE
1/4 CUP CASHEWS, DICED

MIX ALL INGREDIENTS TOGETHER, EXCEPT CASHEWS.
PLACE PORK IN SLOW COOKER, POUR MIXTURE OVER THE
TOP.

COOK ON LOW 8-10 HOURS. TOP WITH CASHEWS WHEN
SERVING.

SERVE ON RICE

SERVINGS: 4-6

The horse knows how to be a horse if we will leave him alone . . . but the riders don't know how to ride. What we should be doing is creating riders and that takes care of the horse immediately. ~Charles de Kunffy

Butterflied Pork Chops

6 BONELESS PORK CHOPS
8-10 RED POTATOES
1 ONION, CHOPPED FINE
1/2 CUP ITALIAN DRESSING
1 PACKET ITALIAN DRESSING MIX
1 TEASPOON BLACK PEPPER
1 GREEN PEPPER, CHOPPED
1 CUP MUSHROOMS, SLICED
PINCH CRUSHED RED PEPPER

POUR ENOUGH SALAD DRESSING TO COVER BOTTOM OF
SLOW COOKER. PLACE 1/2 OF THE ONION IN LIQUID. PUT
PORK ON TOP. MIX ALL OTHER INGREDIENTS THOROUGHLY,
POUR OVER PORK. PLACE POTATOES AROUND PORK. ADD
MUSHROOMS 30 MINUTES BEFORE SERVING.

COOK ON LOW 8-10 HOURS, HIGH 4-6 HOURS.

SERVINGS: 6

*As a horse runs, think of it as a game of tag with the
wind. ~Tre Tuberville*

CHALUPAS

2 POUND PORK LOIN ROAST
1 ONION, CHOPPED FINE
2 TABLESPOONS MINCED GARLIC
3 TABLESPOONS CHILI POWDER
2 TABLESPOONS GROUND CUMIN
1.5 TEASPOONS OREGANO
1 CAN GREEN CHILI PEPPERS, DICED
3 TEASPOONS LIME JUICE
1 JALAPENO, DICED (OPTIONAL)
1 CUP SALSA
1 CAN PINTO OR BLACK BEANS, DRAINED

PLACE PORK IN SLOW COOKER. SET BEANS ASIDE. MIX
TOGETHER ALL OTHER INGREDIENTS. POUR OVER PORK.

COOK ON LOW 8-10 HOURS, HIGH 4-5 HOURS.
1 HOUR BEFORE SERVING ADD BEANS.

SERVINGS: 6

There is no secret so close as that between a rider and his horse. ~Robert Smith Surtees

CARNITAS

1 POUND PORK ROAST
1 TABLESPOON, MINCED GARLIC
2 TEASPOONS JALAPENO, CHOPPED
3 TABLESPOONS TACO SEASONING
1 ONION, CHOPPED
1 TABLESPOON LIME JUICE
1 BUNCH FRESH CILANTRO, CHOPPED
1 BOTTLE OF BEER

PUT PORK IN SLOW COOKER. MIX ALL OTHER INGREDIENTS TOGETHER. POUR OVER PORK.

COOK ON LOW 8-10 HOURS, HIGH 4-6 HOURS

SERVE ON WARM TORTILLAS WITH SALSA, OLIVES, FRESH CHOPPED ONION, AND SOUR CREAM.

SERVINGS: 4-6

When you're young and you fall off a horse, you may break something. When you're my age and you fall off, you splatter. ~Roy Rogers

CHAR SUI PORK

2 POUNDS PORK
1/8 CUP LOW OR NO SODIUM BEEF OR CHICKEN BROTH
1/8 CUP SOY SAUCE
1/4 CUP HOISIN SAUCE
2 TABLESPOONS KETCHUP
2 TABLESPOONS HONEY
1 TEASPOON GARLIC, MINCED
2 TEASPOONS GINGER, GRATED
1 TEASPOON DARK SESAME OIL
1 TEASPOON CHINESE FIVE-SPICE
1 TEASPOON CHILI GARLIC SAUCE
1/4 CUP SLIVERED ALMONDS
1 TEASPOON CORN STARCH

SET ASIDE ALMONDS. PLACE PORK IN SLOW COOKER. MIX
ALL OTHER INGREDIENTS TOGETHER. POUR OVER PORK.

COOK ON LOW 8-10 HOURS, HIGH NOT RECOMMENDED
1 HOUR BEFORE SERVING CREATE CORNSTARCH MIXTURE.
ADD TO SLOW COOKER. TOP WITH ALMONDS WHEN
SERVING. SERVE ON RICE

SERVINGS: 4-6

*He doth nothing but talk of his horses. ~William
Shakespeare*

DIJON PORK

1 PORK LOIN ROAST
1 CLOVE GARLIC, QUARTERED
1 1/4 CUPS BROWN SUGAR, DIVIDED
2 TABLESPOON DIJON MUSTARD
1 TABLESPOON BALSAMIC VINEGAR
1/3 CUP LOW OR NO SODIUM BROTH OR DRY WHITE WINE
1 TEASPOON CINNAMON
1/4 TEASPOON SALT
1 TEASPOON BLACK PEPPER

CUT SLITS INTO ROAST. PUSH GARLIC PIECES INTO SLITS.
PLACE ROAST IN SLOW COOKER. COMBINE ALL OTHER
INGREDIENTS. POUR OVER ROAST.

COOK ON LOW 8-10 HOURS, HIGH NOT RECOMMENDED.
1 HOUR BEFORE SERVING ADD CORNSTARCH MIXTURE TO
THICKEN. TOP WITH SAUCE & BROWN SUGAR.

SERVINGS: 4-6

*Don't be the rider who gallops all night and never sees
the horse that is beneath him. ~Jelaluddin Rumi*

ENCHILADAS CASSEROLE

1 POUND GROUND PORK OR HAMBURGER, BROWNED
1 LARGE CAN ENCHILADA SAUCE
1 ONION, CHOPPED FINE
1 CAN CORN, DRAINED
1 CAN BLACK BEANS, DRAINED
3 CUPS GRATED CHEDDAR CHEESE
1 GREEN OR RED PEPPER, DICED
1 BUNCH CILANTRO, DICED
CORN OR FLOUR TORTILLAS

POUR ENOUGH ENCHILADA SAUCE INTO BOTTOM OF
SLOW COOKER TO COVER. ADD A LAYER OF TORTILLAS.
LAYER OTHER INGREDIENTS BETWEEN TORTILLAS.
CONTINUE LAYERING & TOP WITH ENCHILADA SAUCE
AND CHEESE.

COOK ON LOW 6-8 HOURS, HIGH 3-4 HOURS.

SERVINGS: 4

*Never approach a bull from the front, a horse from the
rear or a fool from any direction. ~Cowboy saying*

MEXICAN MEATLOAF

2 POUNDS GROUND PORK
1.5 CUPS SALSA
1 CUP SHREDDED CHEDDAR CHEESE
1 ONION
1 CAN CORN, DRAINED
1 CAN BLACK BEANS, DRAINED
1-2 TABLESPOONS JALAPENO, CHOPPED FINE (OPTIONAL)
1 EGG
4 CUPS TORTILLA CHIPS, CRUSHED

SPRAY SIDES OF SLOW COOKER WITH COOKING SPRAY OR
BUTTER. SET ASIDE CHEESE. COMBINE ALL INGREDIENTS.
PLACE IN BOTTOM OF SLOW COOKER.

COOK ON LOW 4-5 HOURS, HIGH 3-4 HOURS. 1 HOUR
BEFORE SERVING, SPRINKLE CHEESE ON TOP.

SERVINGS: 6

I've spent most of my life riding horses. The rest I've just wasted. ~Anonymous

PINEAPPLE PORK ROAST

1 PORK ROAST
1 CAN CRUSHED PINEAPPLE, DRAINED
3 TABLESPOONS BROWN SUGAR
3 TABLESPOONS SOY SAUCE
1 CLOVE GARLIC, MINCED
1/2 TEASPOON DRIED BASIL
1 RED PEPPER, CHOPPED
1/4 CUP ALMONDS OR CASHEWS, CHOPPED
1/2 CUP DRY WHITE WINE

PLACE ROAST IN SLOW COOKER. MIX TOGETHER ALL OTHER
INGREDIENTS, EXCEPT ALMONDS. POUR OVER ROAST.
COOK LOW 8-10 HOURS. HIGH NOT RECOMMENDED. 1
HOUR BEFORE SERVING, CREATE A CORNSTARCH MIXTURE,
ADD TO THICKEN JUICES. TOP WITH NUTS WHEN SERVING.
SERVE ON RICE
SERVINGS: 4-6

*He who said he made a small fortune in the horse
business probably started out with a large fortune!
~Anonymous*

The Morgan Horse

The Morgan horse began its journey through history with a man named Justin Morgan. Justin, a composer, businessman, teacher and horseman, acquired a young bay colt who he named Figure. Although Figure's true ancestry is hidden in antiquity, it is believed his sire was True Briton. True Briton was highly respected for producing quality horses. As Figure matured, he became legendary for his beautiful stylish way of moving, his strength, endurance, and for his kind personality. His fame grew throughout the small New England towns where he surpassed other horses' abilities by outdistancing them in every gait, and by pulling better than other breeds of horses. What became most valuable; however, was his aptitude for passing on these traits to his offspring and the generations beyond.

In the mid 1800's, the Morgan breed's ability to trot made it a desirable horse for harness racing. They were used in the Civil War and later for the Pony Express and the U.S. Calvary.

After the Battle of the Little Bighorn, only one member of Custer's military brigade survived, a Morgan-Mustang cross named Comanche.

The Morgan exhibits a strong solid yet refined body, an arched neck, clean throatlatch, chiseled head, expressive large eyes, a distinct wither bone, and a well-placed shoulder. The Morgan Horse Club, now known as the American Morgan Horse Association, was established in 1909 to promote and preserve this breed of horse.

*Donald, an influential Morgan
Stallion, Courtesy of the National
Museum of the Morgan Horse*

Poultry

Apricot Chicken

6 CHICKEN BREASTS
1.5 CUPS APRICOT PRESERVES
1 CUP RUSSIAN DRESSING
1/2 CUP ORANGE MARMALADE
1 ENVELOPE DRY ONION SOUP MIX
1 TEASPOON PEPPER
1/2 TEASPOON DRY MUSTARD

PLACE CHICKEN IN SLOW COOKER. MIX TOGETHER ALL
OTHER INGREDIENTS. POUR OVER CHICKEN. ADD
CORNSTARCH IF NEEDED TO THICKEN JUICES.

COOK ON LOW 5-7 HOURS, HIGH NOT RECOMMENDED.

SERVE OVER RICE.

SERVINGS: 4-6

There are times when you can trust a horse, times when you can't, and times when you have to. ~Anonymous

CHICKEN & DUMPLINGS

2 POUNDS SKINLESS, BONELESS CHICKEN, CUBED
2 TABLESPOONS BUTTER
1 ONION, DICED
3 STALKS CELERY, CHOPPED
2 CANS CREAM OF MUSHROOM SOUP
3 CARROTS, SLICED
1 CUP MUSHROOMS, SLICED
2 PACKAGES REFRIGERATED BISCUIT DOUGH, TORN
INTO PIECES
1/4 CUP LOW OR NO SODIUM CHICKEN BROTH
1/4 CUP DRY WHITE WINE

SET ASIDE BISCUIT DOUGH. PLACE CHICKEN IN SLOW
COOKER. MIX ALL OTHER INGREDIENTS, POUR OVER
CHICKEN. TOP WITH DOUGH.

COOK ON LOW 5-6 HOURS, HIGH NOT RECOMMENDED.

SERVINGS: 4

All I pay my psychiatrist is the cost of feed and hay,
and he'll listen to me any day. ~Anonymous

CREAMY ITALIAN CHICKEN

4 BONELESS SKINLESS CHICKEN BREAST HALVES
1 ENVELOPE ITALIAN SALAD DRESSING MIX
1/2 CUP ITALIAN DRESSING
1 PACKAGE CREAM CHEESE, SOFTENED
1 CAN CONDENSED CREAM OF CHICKEN SOUP
1 CUP FRESH MUSHROOMS, SLICED
1 ONION, CHOPPED FINE
1/2 TEASPOON MINCED GARLIC
2 ZUCCHINI, SLICED

MIX TOGETHER ALL INGREDIENTS. PLACE CHICKEN IN SLOW
COOKER. POUR MIXED INGREDIENTS OVER CHICKEN. ADD
ZUCCHINI 1 HOUR BEFORE SERVING.

COOK ON LOW 3-4 HOURS, HIGH NOT RECOMMENDED

SERVINGS: 4

A lovely horse is always an experience . . . . It is an emotional experience of the kind that is spoiled by words. ~Beryl Markham

CURRIED CHICKEN

6 CHICKEN BONELESS, SKINLESS CHICKEN THIGHS OR
BREASTS
1 TABLESPOONS HOT CURRY PASTE
2 TABLESPOONS YELLOW CURRY POWDER
1/4 CUP LOW OR NO SODIUM CHICKEN BROTH
1 ONION, CHOPPED
1 TABLESPOON SOY SAUCE
1 TABLESPOON GINGER, GRATED
1/2 TEASPOON GINGER POWDER
1 TABLESPOON GARLIC, MINCED

PLACE CHICKEN IN SLOW COOKER. MIX ALL OTHER
INGREDIENTS TOGETHER. POUR OVER CHICKEN.

COOK ON LOW 6-7 HOURS
SERVE ON RICE OR NOODLES

SERVINGS: 6

It's a lot like nuts and bolts—if the rider's nuts, the horse bolts. ~Nicholas Evans

GARLIC CHICKEN & BROCCOLI

2 POUNDS BONELESS, SKINLESS CHICKEN

1/4 CUP LIMEADE

1/4 CUP VINEGAR

3 TABLESPOONS SOY SAUCE

PINCH CRUSHED RED PEPPER

1 CUP BROWN SUGAR

1/2 CUP ONION, CHOPPED FINE

2 CLOVES GARLIC, MINCED

6 LARGE PIECES OF BROCCOLI

PLACE CHICKEN IN SLOW COOKER. STIR TOGETHER ALL
OTHER INGREDIENTS, EXCEPT BROCCOLI. POUR OVER
CHICKEN. THICKEN JUICES WITH 1 TABLESPOON
CORNSTARCH IF NEEDED. ADD BROCCOLI 30 MINUTES
BEFORE SERVING.

COOK ON LOW 6-7 HOURS, HIGH NOT RECOMMENDED

SERVE ON RICE

SERVINGS: 4-6

Riding: The art of keeping a horse between you and the ground. ~Author Unknown

Parmesan Chicken

6 BONELESS CHICKEN BREASTS
1 CAN CREAM OF MUSHROOM SOUP
1 PKG. DRY ONION SOUP MIX
1 TABLESPOON BASIL, CHOPPED
1/4 CUP WHITE OR RED WINE
1 CAN STEWED TOMATOES, UNDRAINED
1 MEDIUM ONION, CHOPPED
1 CUP PARMESAN CHEESE, SHREDDED

PLACE CHICKEN IN SLOW COOKER. COMBINE ALL OTHER INGREDIENTS. POUR OVER CHICKEN.

COOK ON LOW 5-7 HOURS, HIGH 3-4 HOURS. ADD CHEESE LAST 30 MINUTES OF COOKING.
SERVE ON NOODLES.

SERVINGS: 6

If the world was truly a rational place, men would ride side saddle. ~Rita Mae Brown

Sweet & Sour Chicken

3 POUNDS BONELESS, SKINLESS CHICKEN

1 CAN FROZEN LEMONADE, THAWED

1 CAN PINEAPPLE CHUNKS, DRAINED

3 TABLESPOONS BROWN SUGAR

1 GREEN PEPPER, CHOPPED

1/2 ONION, CHOPPED

1 TABLESPOON VINEGAR

4 TABLESPOONS KETCHUP

1/8 TEASPOON SALT

2 TABLESPOONS CORNSTARCH

PLACE CHICKEN INTO SLOW COOKER. COMBINE ALL OTHER INGREDIENTS. POUR OVER CHICKEN.

COOK ON LOW 6-7 HOURS, HIGH NOT RECOMMENDED. 1 HOUR BEFORE SERVING, ADD CORNSTARCH MIXTURE TO THICKEN. SERVE ON RICE.

SERVINGS: 6

Sell the cow, buy the sheep, but never be without the horse. ~Irish Proverb

The American Quarter Horse

In the 17th century early settlers on the east coast of the United States began to breed Thoroughbred horses with the "native" stock, traded or bought from the Indian tribes, or gathered from the wild horse herds. These horses showed a natural "cow sense" or an ability to work cattle. Consequently, they became very popular with cattle ranchers.

Some of the early Texas ranches were instrumental in the development of the American Quarter Horse. The King, the Waggoner, and the 666 ranches developed breeding programs for them. There were many other individuals who can be credited with the early preservation of the Quarter Horse bloodlines, some were racing enthusiasts, others small ranchers.

Often the ranches would compete in informal rivalries with each other. These competitions led to the establishment of the modern day rodeo.

Sprint racing was also a favorite weekend activity in the early towns and cities of America. The Quarter Horse acquired its name because of the ability to out run a Thoroughbred on a quarter mile track.

Today Quarter Horses are known for their abilities in many different riding disciplines: racing, rodeo, reining, cutting, dressage, jumping, gymkhana, and trail riding, just to name a few. In addition, they also make great family horses.

In 1940, the American Quarter Horse Association was founded. Today the American Quarter Horse is the largest breed registry in the world.

Wimpy P-1, photo courtesy of The American Quarter Horse Hall of Fame &
Museum

Vegetarian

BLACK EYED PEAS

1 POUND DRIED BLACK EYED PEAS

6 CUPS WATER

1 TEASPOON GARLIC, MINCED

1 TABLESPOON WHITE WINE VINEGAR

1/2 TEASPOON BLACK PEPPER

1 TABLESPOON BROWN SUGAR

2 OUNCES BACON BITS

1 PACKAGE OF BOCA MEATLESS LINKS, CHOPPED

1 TEASPOON SALT

2 TABLESPOONS BUTTER OR MARGARINE

1 ONION, DICED

1 JALAPENO, DICED (OPTIONAL)

RINSE & SORT BEANS. COMBINE ALL INGREDIENTS IN SLOW COOKER, EXCEPT VINEGAR.

COOK ON LOW 10-12 HOURS, HIGH 5-6 HOURS. ADD VINEGAR WHEN BEANS ARE COOKED THROUGH.

SERVINGS: 6

Horses give us the wings we lack. ~Anonymous

BOLOGNAISE

2 CUPS DRIED SOYBEANS, SOAKED & SORTED
4 LARGE TOMATOES, CUT INTO WEDGES
1 LARGE ONION, CHOPPED
1 POUND OKRA, CHOPPED
1 CUP PITTED GREEN OLIVES, CHOPPED
1 CUP PITTED BLACK OLIVES, CHOPPED
2 CANS TOMATO PASTE
3 CANS PEELED AND DICED TOMATOES, UNDRAINED
1 CUP GRATED PARMESAN CHEESE
1 CUP DRY RED WINE OR LOW OR NO SODIUM BROTH
1/4 CUP OLIVE OIL
1 CAN CORN, DRAINED
3 CARROTS, DICED
2 STALKS CELERY, DICED
2 TABLESPOONS OREGANO
2 TABLESPOONS BASIL
1 TABLESPOON ROSEMARY, CRUSHED
4 TABLESPOONS ITALIAN SEASONING
1/2 TEASPOON SALT
1/2 TEASPOON PEPPER

COMBINE ALL INGREDIENTS, STIR TOGETHER.

COOK ON LOW 10-15 HOURS

SERVINGS: 6

Horses are the dolphins of the plains, the spirits of the wind; yet we sit astride them for the sake of being well groomed, whereas they could have all the desire in the world to bolt, but instead, they adjust their speed and grace, only to please us, never to displease. ~Lauren Salerno

CURRIED RICE WITH LENTILS

1 CUP RICE
1 TABLESPOON CURRY POWDER
1 TEASPOON HOT CURRY PASTE (OPTIONAL)
3/4 CUP LENTILS
1 TABLESPOON GARLIC, MINCED
1/2 TEASPOON BLACK PEPPER
1 ONION, DICED
1 GREEN PEPPER, SLICED
1 RED PEPPER, SLICED
1 PACKAGE MUSHROOMS, SLICED
3.5 CUPS LOW OR NO SODIUM VEGETABLE BROTH

COMBINE INGREDIENTS IN SLOW COOKER.

COOK ON LOW 5-6 HOURS, HIGH 3-4 HOURS.

SERVINGS: 4

I have seen things so beautiful, that they have brought tears to my eyes. Yet, none of them can match the gracefulness and beauty of a horse running free. ~Anonymous

GOULASH

2 PACKAGES MORNINGSTAR GRILLERS
1 ONION, CHOPPED FINE
1 GREEN PEPPER, CHOPPED FINE
2 TEASPOONS GARLIC, MINCED
1 CAN CORN, DRAINED
2 TEASPOONS FRESH BASIL, TORN
1/2 TEASPOON SALT
1 TEASPOON PEPPER
1 LARGE CAN STEWED ITALIAN TOMATOES, DRAINED
1/2 TEASPOON MUSTARD
1/4 CUP KETCHUP

COMBINE ALL INGREDIENTS IN SLOW COOKER. MIX
THOROUGHLY. 1 HOUR BEFORE SERVING MAKE A
ROUX OR CORNSTARCH MIXTURE, ADD TO SLOW COOKER TO
THICKEN JUICES.

COOK ON LOW 6-7 HOURS, HIGH 3-4 HOURS

How to ride a horse: Step One—Mount the horse. Step Two—Stay mounted. ~Anonymous

Italian Eggplant

1 EGGPLANT, CHOPPED INTO BITE SIZED PIECES
1 GREEN PEPPER, CHOPPED
1 ONION, CHOPPED
1 PACKAGE MUSHROOMS, SLICED
1 CAN ITALIAN-STYLE TOMATOES, DRAINED
1 CAN TOMATO PASTE
4 CLOVES GARLIC, MINCED
2 TEASPOONS BROWN SUGAR
1/2 CUP DRY RED WINE OR LOW OR NO SODIUM BROTH
2 TEASPOONS OREGANO
1 CUP PITTED OLIVES
1/2 CUP PARMESAN CHEESE, GRATED
2 TABLESPOONS WALNUTS, CHOPPED FINE
1/2 TEASPOON SALT
1/2 TEASPOON BLACK PEPPER

SET ASIDE MUSHROOMS, CHEESE & NUTS. MIX TOGETHER
ALL OTHER INGREDIENTS.

COOK ON LOW 5-6 HOURS, HIGH 3-4 HOURS. 15
MINUTES BEFORE SERVING, ADD MUSHROOMS & TOP WITH
CHEESE. COOK UNTIL CHEESE IS MELTED.
GARNISH WITH NUTS.

There comes a point in every rider's life when he wonders if it's all worth it. Then one look at the horse, and he realizes—it is. ~Kelly Stewart

Tofu & Squash

3 STALKS CELERY, CHOPPED
1 FENNEL BULB, CHOPPED
3 MEDIUM CARROTS, CHOPPED
1 BUTTERNUT SQUASH, CUBED
2 ZUCCHINI, DICED
2 SUMMER SQUASH, DICED
1 TABLESPOON FRESH GRATED GINGER
PINCH CRUSHED RED PEPPER
1 TEASPOON TURMERIC
2 TABLESPOONS SAFFLOWER OIL
1 TEASPOON GROUND CUMIN
1 TEASPOON GROUND CORIANDER SEED
3 CANS COCONUT MILK
1 TEASPOON SALT
1/2 TEASPOON GROUND BLACK PEPPER
2 TABLESPOONS BACON BITS
2 POUNDS FIRM TOFU
1/2 CUP ALMONDS & WALNUTS, CHOPPED
1 CUP FRESH CILANTRO LEAVES, DICED

SET ASIDE CILANTRO, TOFU & ALMONDS. STIR TOGETHER
ALL OTHER INGREDIENTS IN SLOW COOKER.

COOK ON LOW 4-5 HOURS
30 MINUTES BEFORE SERVING, STIR IN TOFU, & NUTS.
GARNISH WITH CILANTRO.

SERVINGS: 4

You can lead a horse to water but you can't make it drink," is an old saying that is not exactly true, because anybody that's ever been around horses would know if the horse didn't want to go to water then it wouldn't.
~Anonymous

TOFU LASAGNA

2 CANS TOMATO SAUCE

1 CAN CRUSHED TOMATOES, UNDRAINED

2 STALKS CELERY, CHOPPED

1 BELL PEPPER, CHOPPED

1 EGGPLANT, CHOPPED INTO BITE SIZED PIECES

1 TABLESPOON OREGANO

1 TABLESPOON ROSEMARY, DICED

3 CUPS SHREDDED MOZZARELLA CHEESE

1 CONTAINER COTTAGE CHEESE

1 POUND FIRM TOFU, SQUARED

1 PACKAGE NO BOIL LASAGNA NOODLES

1 CUP GRATED PARMESAN CHEESE

SET ASIDE PARMESAN CHEESE. MIX TOMATO SAUCE, TOMATOES & HERBS. COVER BOTTOM OF SLOW COOKER WITH SAUCE. ADD 1 LAYER OF UNCOOKED NOODLES, CONTINUE LAYERING WITH OTHER INGREDIENTS & NOODLES. END WITH SAUCE & CHEESE.

COOK ON LOW 4-6 HOURS

SERVINGS: 4

Fierce as fire and fleet as the wind. ~A.L. Gordon

Spinach & Tofu Marinara Sauce

1 PACKAGE FIRM TOFU, CUBED
1 LARGE CAN CRUSHED TOMATOES, UNDRAINED
1 ONION, CHOPPED
1 CUP CARROTS, DICED
2 CUPS FRESH SPINACH, CHOPPED
4 CLOVES GARLIC, MINCED
2 CANS TOMATO PASTE
1 PACKAGE MUSHROOMS, SLICED
1 TEASPOON SALT
2 TABLESPOONS ITALIAN SEASONINGS
2 TABLESPOONS ROSEMARY
3 TABLESPOONS RED PEPPER
2 BAY LEAVES

IN SLOW COOKER MIX TOGETHER ALL INGREDIENTS.

COOK ON LOW 4-6 HOURS, HIGH 3-4 HOURS. REMOVE BAY LEAVES. SERVE ON NOODLES.

SERVINGS: 4

Horses can't talk, but they can speak if you listen.
~Anonymous.

STUFFED SQUASH

4 SUMMER SQUASH HALVED, SEEDS REMOVED
1 TABLESPOON ITALIAN SEASONING
1 SMALL CAN TOMATO SAUCE
1 ONION, CHOPPED FINE
1 TEASPOON MINCED GARLIC
1/2 CUP COOKED BROWN RICE
1 TABLESPOON FRESH BASIL, MINCED
1/4 TEASPOON BLACK PEPPER
2 TABLESPOONS RED WINE VINEGAR
3 TABLESPOONS PINE NUTS OR SUNFLOWER SEEDS
1 CUP MOZZARELLA CHEESE, GRATED
1/2 CUP PARMESAN CHEESE, GRATED
1/4 CUP GORGONZOLA CHEESE, CRUMBLES
FRESH PARSLEY FOR GARNISH

PUT SQUASH IN SLOW COOKER. COMBINE VINEGAR &
TOMATO SAUCE, SET ASIDE. CREATE A MIXTURE WITH
OTHER INGREDIENTS. STUFF SQUASH WITH RICE MIXTURE,
TOP WITH VINEGAR MIXTURE.

COOK ON LOW 2-3 HOURS, HIGH 1-2 HOURS.
15 MINUTES BEFORE SERVING, TOP WITH CHEESES.
GARNISH WITH PARSLEY & PINE NUTS.

SERVINGS: 4

When God wanted to create the horse, he said to the South Wind, "I want to make a creature of you. Condense. And the Wind condensed."
~Emir Abd-el-Kader

Vegetarian Chow Mein

1 POUND SEITAN, CHOPPED

6 GREEN ONIONS, SLICED

2 CARROTS, DICED

1 CUP BUTTON MUSHROOMS

2 STALKS CELERY, CHOPPED

1 CUP BROCCOLI, CHOPPED

1.5 CUPS LOW OR NO SODIUM VEGETABLE BROTH

1/4 CUP SOY SAUCE (LOW SODIUM)

1 TEASPOON FRESH GINGER, GRATED

1/4 TEASPOON RED PEPPER

1 CUP BEAN SPROUTS

1 CAN WATER CHESTNUTS, SLICED

2 TABLESPOONS CORNSTARCH

MIX INGREDIENTS TOGETHER IN SLOW COOKER.

COOK ON LOW 4-6 HOURS. 1 HOUR BEFORE SERVING MAKE & ADD CORNSTARCH MIXTURE. SERVE ON RICE OR NOODLES.

SERVINGS: 6

How do you catch a loose horse? Make a noise like a carrot. ~British Cavalry joke

The American Paint Horse

In 1519 the explorer from Spain, Hernando Cortes, came to America looking for fame and riches. From across the sea, he brought conquistadors and horses with him to the new world. According to a historian who traveled with the group, two pintos were among them.

Later, many of the spotted horses populated the herds of mustangs that dotted the open plains. They soon became a favorite of the American Indian. The Comanche, believed by many to be the master horseman of the plains, had a great attraction to the pinto colored horses.

The paint breed was developed using the spotted pattern of the mustang combined with Quarter horse and Thoroughbred blood.

When the American Quarter Horse Association was created, it rejected horses with pinto markings or "crop out" horses, those with spots on their bodies or white above the knees and hocks.

In May 1965, a number of groups dedicated to preserving these spotted horses united to become the American Paint Horse Association.

Today Paints are extremely popular and excel at many different disciplines. Horse racing, gymkhana, cutting, reining, jumping, rodeo, and trail riding, are just a few of the sports that this breed of horse competes in.

Photograph courtesy of the
American Paint Horse Association

Seafood

Catfish in Wine Sauce

1 POUND CATFISH OR OTHER WHITE MEAT FISH
1 CAN OF CREAM OF CELERY SOUP
1/4 CUP DRY WHITE WINE OR LOW OR NO SODIUM
VEGETABLE BROTH
2 CUPS DICED POTATOES
1 CUP GRATED PARMESAN CHEESE
1 TABLESPOON PARSLEY, CHOPPED
1/4 TEASPOON SALT
1 TEASPOON DRIED BASIL
1 TEASPOON DRIED OREGANO

MIX WINE & SOUP TOGETHER. COVER BOTTOM OF SLOW
COOKER WITH MIXTURE. ADD POTATOES, FISH, TOP WITH
SEASONINGS. FINISH WITH CHEESE.

COOK ON LOW 2-3 HOURS OR UNTIL FISH IS JUST COOKED
THROUGH.

SERVINGS: 3-4

If you want a stable friendship, get a horse. ~Anonymous

CIOPINNO

1 POUND SEA BASS, CUT INTO BITE SIZED PIECES
2 CUPS MUSHROOMS, SLICED
3 CARROTS, SLICED
1 ONION, CHOPPED
1 GREEN PEPPER, CHOPPED
1 TEASPOON GARLIC, MINCED
2 CUPS TOMATO SAUCE
2 CUPS LOW OR NO SODIUM BEEF BROTH
1/2 TEASPOON SALT
1/2 TEASPOON PEPPER
1 TEASPOON OREGANO
1 CAN CLAMS, UNDRAINED
1 POUND SHRIMP
1 PACKAGE CRAB MEAT
1 TABLESPOON MINCED PARSLEY
2 LEMONS, SQUEEZED

PLACE ALL INGREDIENTS IN SLOW COOKER. MIX
THOROUGHLY.

COOK ON LOW 4-5 HOURS

SERVINGS: 6

I used to have money, now I have horses. ~Most of Us

CITRUS ZEST FISH

4 FISH FILLETS
1/4 CUP LIMEADE
1/4 CUP ORANGE JUICE
1/2 JALAPEÑO PEPPER, SEEDED **&** MINCED (OPTIONAL)
1 LARGE PIECE GINGER ROOT, DICED
1 TABLESPOON OLIVE OIL
1/2 TEASPOON SALT
1/4 TEASPOON BLACK PEPPER
1/2 TEASPOON LEMON PEPPER
1/8 CUP CILANTRO, DICED

PLACE FISH INSIDE SLOW COOKER. COMBINE ALL OTHER INGREDIENTS, EXCEPT CILANTRO. POUR OVER FISH.

COOK ON LOW **3-4** HOURS, HIGH **2-3** HOURS OR UNTIL FISH IS COOKED THROUGH. GARNISH WITH LEMON WEDGES **&** CILANTRO.

SERVINGS: **4**

Love means attention, which means looking after the things we love. We call this stable management.
~George H. Morris

CLAM & SHRIMP BAKE

3 CANS MINCED CLAMS, DRAINED
2 CANS BABY SHRIMP, DRAINED
4 EGGS, BEATEN
1/2 CUP BUTTER, MELTED
1/4 CUP MILK
1/4 ONION, MINCED
1 STALK CELERY, MINCED
20 RITZ CRACKERS, CRUSHED

BUTTER SIDES OF SLOW COOKER OR SPRAY WITH NONSTICK COOKING SPRAY. COMBINE ALL INGREDIENTS.

COOK ON LOW 4-5 HOURS, HIGH NOT RECOMMENDED

SERVINGS: 4

My husband says, if I spend one more weekend at a horse-show, he'll leave me. Darn—I'll miss him.
~Anonymous

CAJUN SHRIMP

2 POUNDS COOKED SHRIMP
1 TABLESPOON BUTTER, MELTED
1/2 CUP WATER
1/2 CUP DRY RED WINE
1 ONION, MINCED
2 TABLESPOONS DRY BUTTERMILK BISCUIT MIX
1 SMALL CAN STEWED TOMATOES, UNDRAINED
1 SMALL CAN TOMATO PASTE
2 TABLESPOONS CAJUN SEASONING
1/2 TEASPOON SUGAR
1 BAY LEAF
1 JALAPENO PEPPER, MINCED (OPTIONAL)
2 STALKS CELERY, CHOPPED
1 GREEN PEPPER, CHOPPED

COMBINE ALL LIQUIDS IN SLOW COOKER. ADD BISCUIT MIX, SUGAR AND THEN ALL OTHER INGREDIENTS.

COOK ON LOW 4-5 HOURS, HIGH 2-3 HOURS

SERVINGS: 3-4

Life is short. Hug your horse. ~Anonymous

Halibut in Wine Sauce

2 HALIBUT STEAKS
1/2 CUP HALF & HALF
1/2 CUP BUTTER, MELTED
1/4 CUP DRY WHITE WINE
1/4 TEASPOON SALT
1 TABLESPOON BROWN SUGAR
2 TABLESPOONS CILANTRO, MINCED
1 PINCH OF CHILI POWDER
1 TABLESPOON CORNSTARCH

PLACE HALIBUT IN SLOW COOKER. ADD CORNSTARCH
TO BUTTER, MIX THOROUGHLY. COMBINE WITH OTHER
INGREDIENTS. POUR OVER FISH.

COOK ON LOW 3-4 HOURS, HIGH NOT RECOMMENDED

SERVINGS: 2

A Hibernian sage once wrote that there are three things a man never forgets: The girl of his early youth, a devoted teacher, and a great horse. ~C.J.J. Mullen

POACHED SALMON

4 BONELESS SALMON FILLETS
1-8 OZ. PACKAGE OF BRIE CHEESE
3 TABLESPOONS ROSEMARY, DICED
1/2 ONION, CHOPPED FINE
4 LEMONS
1 TEASPOON SEAFOOD SEASONING
1 POUND COOKED SHRIMP, DICED

SQUEEZE LEMON JUICE TO COVER BOTTOM OF SLOW
COOKER. SOFTEN BRIE CHEESE, MIX WITH OTHER
INGREDIENTS. CUT A DEEP HORIZONTAL SLIT IN EACH
FILLET, STUFF WITH CHEESE MIXTURE.

COOK ON LOW 3-4 HOURS, HIGH 2-3 HOURS OR UNTIL
FISH IS COOKED THROUGH. SERVE WITH RICE.

SERVINGS: 4

About the head of a truly great horse there is an air of freedom unconquerable. The eyes seem to look on heights beyond our gaze. It is the look of a spirit that can soar. ~John Taintor Foote

Scallops in White Sauce

1 POUND SCALLOPS
1/4 CUP BUTTER, MELTED
1/4 CUP DRY WHITE WINE
1 TABLESPOON CILANTRO, MINCED
2 TABLESPOONS PARSLEY, MINCED
1 TABLESPOON SHALLOTS, CHOPPED
2 TABLESPOONS PALE DRY SHERRY
1 PACKAGE MUSHROOMS, SLICED

COMBINE ALL INGREDIENTS IN SLOW COOKER. SET ASIDE 1/2 OF MUSHROOMS & BUTTER.

COOK ON LOW 4-5 HOURS OR UNTIL FISH IS COOKED THROUGH. MAKE ROUX WITH 1 TEASPOON FLOUR & BUTTER. 30 MINUTES BEFORE SERVING, ADD REMAINING MUSHROOMS & ROUX. MIX GENTLY, BUT THOROUGHLY.

SERVINGS: 2

My new horse was sold to me as a real gentleman to ride. He is. When we have to go over a fence, he insists on "ladies first." ~Anonymous

Seafood Gumbo

1 POUND RAW SHRIMP

1 POUND CRAB MEAT

3 PIECES COOKED BACON, DICED

3 STALKS CELERY, SLICED

1 ONION, CHOPPED

1 GREEN PEPPER, CHOPPED

3 GARLIC CLOVES, MINCED

2 CUPS LOW OR NO SODIUM CHICKEN BROTH

1/2 CUP DRY WHITE WINE

1 CAN DICED TOMATOES, DRAINED

3 TABLESPOONS WORCESTERSHIRE SAUCE

1 TABLESPOON HOT SAUCE

1/2 CUP CILANTRO, DICED

1 TEASPOON SALT OR TO TASTE

1 TEASPOON THYME

3 POUNDS OKRA, CHOPPED

2 CUPS COOKED RICE

SET RICE ASIDE. COMBINE ALL OTHER INGREDIENTS. COOK ON LOW 3-4 HOURS, HIGH NOT RECOMMENDED. 30 MINUTES BEFORE SERVING ADD RICE.

SERVINGS: 4-6

You know your a horseperson when your horse gets shoes more often than you do.~Anonymous

TUNA CASSEROLE

2 CANS TUNA FISH, DRAINED
3 SLICES TOASTED BREAD, TORN INTO SMALL PIECES
1/2 CUP DRY WHITE WINE OR MILK
1 CAN CREAM OF MUSHROOM SOUP
1/2 CUP POTATO CHIPS, BROKEN INTO SMALL PIECES
3 STALKS CELERY, CHOPPED
2 CUPS MUSHROOMS, SLICED

SET POTATO CHIPS, MUSHROOMS & CELERY ASIDE.
COMBINE ALL OTHER INGREDIENTS. POUR INTO BUTTERED
SLOW COOKER.

COOK ON LOW 4-5 HOURS. LAST 30 MINUTES OF
COOKING ADD CELERY & MUSHROOMS. TOP WITH POTATO
CHIPS WHEN SERVING. SERVE ON NOODLES.

SERVINGS: 4

If the horse does not enjoy his work, his rider will have no joy. ~H.H. Isenbart

The American Saddlebred

The American Saddlebred is a horse with a high stepping gait, long sloping shoulder, high arched neck, an intelligent face, and an elegant carriage. They were originally created by crossing the Thoroughbred and the Narragansett pacer. In the early days of their evolution, they were known as the American Horse, and over time became popular in Kentucky as an easy, comfortable, ground covering plantation horse. They were capable of hard work on the farm, races on the weekends, and were fancy enough to pull the carriage into town. In Kentucky they were celebrated as the Kentucky Saddler. Later Morgan blood was added to the breed, and this new creation became the American Saddlebred.

One of the things that make them unique is the fact that they can execute five gaits rather than the normal three that most breeds of horses display.

In their early inception, Saddlebreds carried many famous individuals into the civil war. Lee, Sherman, Grant, Stonewall Jackson, John Hunt Morgan and Nathan Bedford Forrest all rode American Saddlebreds.

Because of their popularity and commercial value a registry was formed. In 1891, the American Saddle-Horse Breeders' Association was created in Louisville, Kentucky. In 1980, the name was changed to American Saddlebred Horse Association.

The Saddlebred is still very popular today as a show horse, with the original purpose of them being a breed that works successfully in many different disciplines with style.

Many famous Hollywood stars were Saddlebreds: The stars of My Friend Flicka, Mr. Ed, Gone With The Wind and National Velvet were all flashy American Saddlebred horses.

American Saddlebred Breeding Stallion, Bourbon, Artist: George Ford Morris, Courtesy Of The American Saddlebred Museum

Side Dishes

ASPARAGUS CASSEROLE

1 BUNCH ASPARAGUS, CHOPPED
1 CAN CREAM OF CELERY SOUP
2 HARD-BOILED EGGS, SLICED
1/2 ONION, CHOPPED, FINE
2 CUPS SHREDDED CHEDDAR CHEESE
1 CUP RITZ CRACKERS, CRUSHED
1 TEASPOON BUTTER
2 TABLESPOONS DRY WHITE WINE
1/2 CUP FINELY CHOPPED WALNUTS

IN BOWL MIX TOGETHER WINE, ASPARAGUS & SOUP. POUR
INTO BUTTERED SLOW COOKER. LAYER EGGS, CHEESE,
NUTS & THEN CRACKERS. DOT WITH BUTTER.

COOK ON LOW 3-4 HOURS, HIGH NOT RECOMMENDED.

SERVINGS: 2-3

*A polo pony is like a motorbike with a mind of its own,
weighing half a ton. ~Anonymous*

BAKED BEANS

2 POUNDS DRIED BEANS (SOAKED OVERNIGHT & SORTED)
2 ONIONS, QUARTERED
6 WHOLE CLOVES
1 CUP LIGHT MOLASSES
2 TABLESPOONS BROWN SUGAR
1 TABLESPOON SALT
1 TABLESPOON DRY MUSTARD
1/2 POUND BACON, COOKED & DICED
1/4 CUP APPLE CIDER VINEGAR

STUD ONIONS WITH CLOVES. PLACE IN BOTTOM OF
SLOW COOKER. SET ASIDE VINEGAR. MIX ALL OTHER
INGREDIENTS TOGETHER WITH 1 CUP WATER. STIR INTO
BEANS. ADD TO SLOW COOKER. POUR ENOUGH WATER ON
TOP TO COVER BEANS. ADD VINEGAR ONE HOUR BEFORE
SERVING. BEANS MUST BE COOKED TROUGH BEFORE
VINEGAR IS ADDED.

COOK ON LOW 8-10 HOURS, HIGH NOT RECOMMENDED

SERVINGS: 8-10

A bad day riding is better than a good day fishing.
~Anonymous

Macaroni & Cheese

1/2 POUND UNCOOKED MACARONI PASTA
1 CAN EVAPORATED MILK
1-1/4 CUPS MILK
1 EGG
1 CONTAINER ALFREDO SAUCE (10 OZ.)
2 TABLESPOONS DIJON MUSTARD
4 CUPS SHREDDED CHEDDAR CHEESE
1/4 CUP GRATED PARMESAN CHEESE
3 TABLESPOONS BUTTER, MELTED
1/8 TEASPOON WHITE PEPPER
1/2 TEASPOON ONION POWDER
1/8 TEASPOON GARLIC POWDER
1/2 TEASPOON SALT

COAT SLOW COOKER WITH BUTTER. MIX ALL INGREDIENTS
TOGETHER. POUR INTO SLOW COOKER.

COOK ON LOW 3-4 HOURS

SERVINGS: 4-6

One way to stop a runaway horse is to bet on him.
~Jeffrey Bernard

Refried Beans

1 ONION, DICED
3 CUPS DRY PINTO BEANS, SOAKED, RINSED & SORTED
1 JALAPENO PEPPER, CHOPPED (OPTIONAL)
3 TABLESPOONS MINCED GARLIC
1 TEASPOON SALT
2 TEASPOONS BLACK PEPPER
1 TEASPOON GROUND CUMIN
8 CUPS WATER

POUR ALL INGREDIENTS IN SLOW COOKER.

COOK ON LOW 8-10 HOURS, HIGH 5-6 HOURS. AFTER
COOKING, DRAIN. MASH BEANS WITH A POTATO MASHER,
ADDING WATER, AS NEEDED. FRY BEANS IN BACON GREASE
OR VEGETABLE OIL.

SERVINGS: 4-6

*Whoever said money can't buy happiness didn't know
where to buy a horse. ~Anonymous*

RICE

2 CUPS JASMINE RICE
4 CUPS WATER
1 TEASPOON SALT
2 TABLESPOONS BUTTER OR OLIVE OIL

COAT SIDES & BOTTOM OF SLOW COOKER WITH BUTTER OR OIL. COMBINE ALL INGREDIENTS IN SLOW COOKER.

COOK ON LOW 4-6 HOURS, HIGH NOT RECOMMENDED.

SERVINGS: 4-6

A horse doesn't care how much you know until he knows how much you care. ~Pat Parelli

Roasted Vegetables

4 carrots cut into bite sized chunks
4 russet potatoes, scrubbed, chopped
3 stalks celery, chopped
1 onion, chopped
1 package mushrooms, sliced
2 cloves garlic, minced
3 tablespoons water
2 tablespoons olive oil
1/4 teaspoon salt
1/4 teaspoon pepper
1 teaspoon mrs. dash

Set aside celery & mushrooms. Combine all other ingredients in slow cooker. 30 minutes before serving add celery & mushrooms.

Cook on low 2-4 hours

Servings: 4

You cannot train a horse with shouts and expect it to obey a whisper. ~Anonymous

SCALLOPED POTATOES

5 POTATOES, SCRUBBED THOROUGHLY, SLICED
1.5 CUPS MILK OR HALF & HALF
2 TABLESPOONS BUTTER
2 ONIONS, CHOPPED
1 TEASPOON SALT
1 TEASPOON BLACK PEPPER
1 TABLESPOON PAPRIKA

COAT SIDES & BOTTOM OF SLOW COOKER WITH BUTTER.
LAYER MILK, POTATOES, ONIONS, BUTTER, SALT, PEPPER.
TOP WITH PAPRIKA.

COOK ON LOW 4-6 HOURS, HIGH NOT RECOMMENDED. 1
HOUR BEFORE SERVING MAKE A ROUX, ADD GENTLY TO
THICKEN.

SERVINGS: 8-10

*A Dog looks up to a man, a cat looks down on a man,
but a patient horse looks a man in the eye and sees him
as an equal. ~Anonymous*

STEAMED VEGETABLES

4 CARROTS, CHOPPED
8 BROCCOLI CROWNS, CHOPPED
3 STALKS CELERY, CHOPPED
1 ONION, CHOPPED
1 CLOVE GARLIC, MINCED
4 TABLESPOONS WATER
1 PACKAGE MUSHROOMS, CHOPPED
3 SUMMER SQUASH, CHOPPED
1/4 TEASPOON SALT
1/4 TEASPOON PEPPER

SET ASIDE CELERY AND MUSHROOMS. COMBINE ALL OTHER
INGREDIENTS IN SLOW COOKER. 30 MINUTES BEFORE
SERVING ADD CELERY AND MUSHROOMS TO DISH.

COOK ON LOW 3-4 HOURS, HIGH 2-3 HOURS

SERVINGS: 3-4

A horse is like a violin. First it must be tuned, and when tuned, it must be accurately played. ~Anonymous

STUFFING

12 CUPS TOASTED BREAD CUBES

1 PACKAGE FRESH MUSHROOMS, QUARTERED

1 STICK BUTTER, MELTED

3 TABLESPOONS POULTRY SEASONING

2 EGGS, BEATEN

2 CUPS ONION, CHOPPED FINE

2 CUPS CELERY, CHOPPED

1 APPLE, DICED

1 TABLESPOON SAGE

1/2 TEASPOON SALT

1/2 TEASPOON PEPPER

1.5 CUPS LOW OR NO SODIUM CHICKEN BROTH

COMBINE ALL INGREDIENTS IN SLOW COOKER. MIX THOROUGHLY.

COOK ON LOW **2-3** HOURS, HIGH NOT RECOMMENDED

SERVINGS: **4-6**

A horse is an angel without wings. ~Anonymous

SWEET POTATO

4 SWEET POTATOES, CHOPPED
1/2 CUP BROWN SUGAR
1/2 CUP COCONUT, FLAKED
1/2 CUP MELTED BUTTER
1/2 CUP CHOPPED PECANS
1/2 TEASPOON VANILLA
1/2 TEASPOON CINNAMON
1/4 CUP DATES, DICED

COAT SLOW COOKER WITH BUTTER. SET ASIDE VANILLA.
MIX TOGETHER ALL OTHER INGREDIENTS. TOP WITH DATES.

COOK ON LOW 5-8 HOURS, HIGH NOT RECOMMENDED.
STIR IN VANILLA WHEN COOKING HAS ENDED.

SERVINGS: 4-6

A horse is like a best friend. They're always there to nuzzle you and make your life a better place.
~Anonymous

WILD RICE

2 CUPS UNCOOKED WILD RICE
1/2 TEASPOON SALT
1/8 TEASPOON PEPPER
4.5 CUPS WATER OR LOW OR NO SODIUM CHICKEN BROTH
1 TEASPOON DRIED THYME LEAVES

STIR ALL INGREDIENTS TOGETHER IN SLOW COOKER.

COOK ON LOW 4-6 HOURS, HIGH 3-4 HOURS.

SERVINGS: 4-6

A dog may be man's best friend, but the horse wrote history. ~Anonymous

Draft Horses

By the 19th century, tall, heavily muscled, horses with mighty strength were needed for agriculture, transportation, and many forms of heavy pulling. This horsepower moved from Europe, across the oceans, to the United States in the late 1800's. France sent Percherons, Belgians came from Belgium, England furnished Shires, and Scotland supplied Clydesdales. By the late 1800's, all of these breeds had established breed registries.

These large horses were used for daily jobs of labor. Their strength was also needed during the first world war for military purposes. After the second world war, machines were introduced that replaced the draft horse. The railroads, tractors and other forms of machinery made the need for these big animals obsolete, consequently, their popularity declined. However, in the present day, they are still used by the Mennonite and Amish agriculturalists.

The American Cream Draft, is the only breed of draft horse that was created and bred exclusively in the United States.

Shows featuring heavy hauling and driving competitions currently support the draft horses' popularity.

Many of today's Olympic and FEI level horses are warmbloods. These breeds were created by crossing the cold blooded draft horses with the hot blooded breeds such as Thoroughbreds and Arabians.

Fifth place—Laet 133886
Grand champion stallion, International, 1921
Owned by W. H. Butler, 17 S. High St., Columbus, Ohio

Photograph courtesy of the
Percheron Horse Association

Desserts

Apple Cobbler

4 TART APPLES, DICED
1/2 CUP BROWN SUGAR
3 TABLESPOONS BUTTER
1 CUP GRANOLA CEREAL WITH FRUIT AND NUTS
1 TEASPOON CINNAMON
1/4 CUP CHOPPED WALNUTS

COAT THE SIDES OF THE SLOW COOKER WITH BUTTER OR NON-STICK COOKING SPRAY. COMBINE ALL INGREDIENTS AND POUR INTO SLOW COOKER.

COOK ON LOW 3-5 HOURS, HIGH NOT RECOMMENDED

SERVINGS: 4

Nothing moves me more—when on the way to fetching in my mare in the morning—than the sound of her neighing to me as I open the gate. ~Anonymous

APPLE PIE

10 TART APPLES, SLICED
2 TEASPOONS CINNAMON
1/2 TEASPOON ALLSPICE
1/2 TEASPOON NUTMEG
3/4 CUP MILK
2 EGGS
1/4 CUP DARK BROWN SUGAR
1 TEASPOON VANILLA
1.5 CUPS BISQUICK
4 TABLESPOONS BUTTER, SOFTENED

BUTTER SLOW COOKER. MIX TOGETHER APPLES & SPICES. POUR APPLE MIXTURE INTO SLOW COOKER. MIX MILK, EGGS, VANILLA, & 1/2 CUP BISQUICK. POUR OVER APPLES. STIR TOGETHER REMAINING BISQUICK, SUGAR & BUTTER UNTIL CRUMBLY. POUR OVER APPLES.

COOK ON LOW 5-6 HOURS, HIGH NOT RECOMMENDED

SERVINGS: 6-8

Alimony is like buying hay for a dead horse. ~Groucho Marx

BANANA NUT BREAD

1 CUP RIPE MASHED BANANA
1/2 CUP PINEAPPLE/BANANA JUICE
1 TEASPOON CINNAMON
1/2 CUP SUGAR
4 TABLESPOONS BUTTER, MELTED
2 EGGS
1 TEASPOON VANILLA
1 TEASPOON BAKING POWDER
1/4 TEASPOON BAKING SODA
1 CUP WALNUTS, CHOPPED
2 CUPS FLOUR

BUTTER & FLOUR INSERT. POUR MIXTURE UNTIL 1/2 FULL.
ROLL 3-4 ALUMINUM BALLS & PLACE UNDER INSERT TO
ALLOW AIR FLOW. FROST WHEN COOL (OPTIONAL).

COOK ON HIGH 4-6 HOURS.

SERVINGS: 4

To many, the words love, hope, and dreams are synonymous with horses. ~Oliver Wendell Holmes

CARAMEL & APPLES

4 TART APPLES, CORED
16 CARAMELS, UNWRAPPED
1 TEASPOON CINNAMON
1 TEASPOON GRATED FRESH GINGER
2 TABLESPOONS WATER

BUTTER THE SIDES AND BOTTOM OF THE SLOW COOKER.
POUR WATER IN BOTTOM. ADD THE APPLES, THEN PLACE
4 CARAMELS IN EACH APPLE. SPRINKLE 1/4 AMOUNT OF
CINNAMON AND THEN GINGER OVER CARAMELS IN EACH
APPLE.

COOK ON LOW 3-4 HOURS, HIGH 1-2 HOURS.

SERVINGS: 4

When riding a horse, we leave our fear, troubles, and
sadness behind on the ground. ~Juli Carlson

CARAMEL CUSTARD

6 EGGS
2 CUPS MILK
1/4 CUP DARK BROWN SUGAR
1 TABLESPOON VANILLA
10-12 CARAMELS, UNWRAPPED

BUTTER SIDES AND BOTTOM OF SLOW COOKER. MIX EGGS, MILK, SUGAR, & VANILLA TOGETHER. POUR INTO SLOW COOKER.

COOK ON LOW 6-8 HOURS, HIGH NOT RECOMMENDED. WHEN TOP OF CUSTARD IS FIRM, PLACE CARAMELS ON TOP. COOK UNTIL MELTED.

SERVINGS: 4

Who among us has not as a child asked Santa Clause to bring us a pony on Christmas day? ~Anonymous

CHOCOLATE CAKE

1 PACKAGE CHOCOLATE CAKE MIX
1 PACKAGE INSTANT CHOCOLATE PUDDING
5 EGGS
1 CUP WATER
3/4 CUP VEGETABLE OIL
1.5 CUPS SOUR CREAM
1 CUP ALMONDS, CHOPPED

BUTTER & FLOUR INSERT. MIX ALL INGREDIENTS
TOGETHER. POUR INTO INSERT TO 1/2 FULL. PLACE IN
SLOW COOKER ON 3 BALLS OF ALUMINUM FOIL FOR AIR
FLOW.

COOK ON HIGH 6-7 HOURS, SPOON INTO BOWLS.

SERVINGS: 6-8

When your horse follows you without being asked, when he rubs his head on yours, and when you look at him and feel a tingle down your spine you, know you are loved. Do you love him back? ~Anonymous

PEACH COBBLER

6 FRESH PEACHES, SLICED
1 CUP OATS
1/2 CUP FLOUR
1/4 CUP BROWN SUGAR
1/4 TEASPOON NUTMEG
1 TEASPOON VANILLA
1 TEASPOON GROUND CINNAMON
1/2 CUP SOFTENED BUTTER

COAT INSIDE OF SLOW COOKER WITH BUTTER OR NONSTICK
COOKING SPRAY. PUT PEACHES IN BOTTOM. MIX
TOGETHER ALL OTHER INGREDIENTS, POURING BUTTER
INTO MIXTURE SLOWLY UNTIL CRUMBLY. POUR ON TOP OF
PEACHES.

COOK ON LOW 2-3 HOURS, HIGH NOT RECOMMENDED

SERVINGS: 4

*To understand the soul of a horse is the closest we
humans can come to knowing perfection ~Anonymous*

Pears in Wine

6 PEARS, PEELED
1/2 TEASPOON NUTMEG
1/2 BOTTLE OF RED WINE
3 CUPS ORANGE JUICE
8 WHOLE CLOVES
ZEST OF 2 ORANGES
1/2 TEASPOON CINNAMON
1 TEASPOON VANILLA
1.5 CUPS SUGAR

STAND PEARS IN SLOW COOKER, CUT BOTTOMS TO FLATTEN IF NEEDED. COMBINE ALL OTHER INGREDIENTS. POUR OVER PEARS.

COOK ON LOW 2-3 HOURS, HIGH 1-2 HOURS. SERVE CHILLED WITH WHIPPING CREAM.

SERVINGS: 6

When riding my horse, I no longer have my heart in my chest, but between my knees. ~Anonymous

PUMPKIN CAKE

2 CUPS OF PUMPKIN
2 EGGS
3 TEASPOONS CINNAMON
1/2 TEASPOON NUTMEG
1/2 TEASPOON CLOVES
1/2 TEASPOON GINGER
1 TEASPOON BAKING SODA
2 TEASPOONS BAKING POWDER
1 CUP OF OIL
1/2 CUP OF ORANGE JUICE
1 CUP + 2 TABLESPOONS BROWN SUGAR
2 3/4 CUPS FLOUR
1 CUP WALNUTS, CHOPPED

BUTTER & FLOUR INSERT. IN BOWL, MIX ALL INGREDIENTS
TOGETHER. POUR INTO INSERT TO 1/2 FULL. SPRINKLE 2
TABLESPOONS SUGAR ON TOP. PLACE IN SLOW COOKER ON
3 ALUMINUM FOIL BALLS FOR AIRFLOW.

COOK ON HIGH 3-4 HOURS. THIS RECIPE MAKES 2 LOAF
PAN SIZED CAKES.

SERVINGS: 10-12

There is nothing like a rattling ride for curing melancholy! ~Pared

Rice Pudding

1/4 GALLON WHOLE MILK
1 CUP SUGAR
1 CUP UNCOOKED RICE
1/4 TEASPOON SALT
2 TEASPOONS VANILLA
4 EGGS
1/4 CUP RAISINS OR CHOPPED DATES

MIX ALL INGREDIENTS TOGETHER IN BOWL. COAT THE
SIDES AND BOTTOM OF SLOW COOKER WITH BUTTER. POUR
RICE MIXTURE INTO SLOW COOKER.

COOK ON LOW 2-4 HOURS, STIRRING OCCASIONALLY. HIGH
NOT RECOMMENDED.

SERVINGS: 4-6

Look back at our struggle for freedom, Trace our present day's strength to its source; And you'll find that man's pathway to glory Is strewn with the bones of the horse. ~Author Unknown

The Tennessee Walking Horse

In the late 1800's, plantation horses were needed in the south that were hardy enough to be ridden all day, would maintain an even temper, could cover a lot of ground quickly, and be smooth to ride. In the state of Tennessee, breeders blended the blood of the Canadian Pacer and the Narragansett Pacer and thus, the Tennessee Walking Horse began its journey into the history books of America. Later in the evolution of this breed, Thoroughbred, Standardbred, Morgan, American Saddlebred, Confederate Pacer and Union Trotter were bloodlines that helped to refine while adding great vigor to the breed.

The Tennessee Walking Horse has three unique smooth gaits, that made it an ideal plantation horse. These gaits are: the flat-foot walk, running walk, and the canter.

Many of these horses were used for working during the week, and racing on the weekends. As these horses gained popularity, breeders began to refine them, creating showier mounts.

A Registry, called The Tennessee Walking Horse Breeders' & Exhibitors' Association, was formed in 1935.

Today, the Tennessee Walking Horse is known for having a kind and gentle disposition, and they are highly sought after for trail riding.

The Tennessee Walking Horse is known for being a smooth gaited, refined, tough breed of horse with a great deal of stamina.

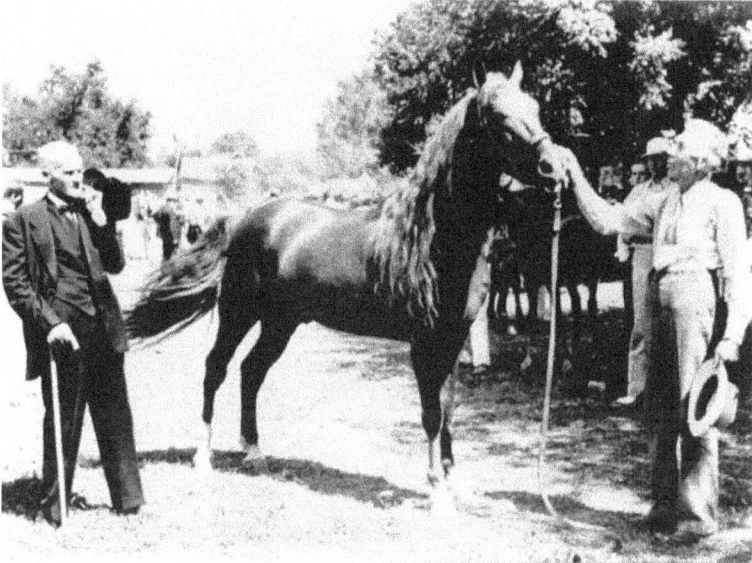

*Photo courtesy of: The Tennessee
Walking Horse Breeders' and
Exhibitors' Association*

Horse Treats

Breakfast Bran Treats

3 CUPS BRAN CEREAL FLAKES
1 CUP APPLE JUICE
1/4 CUP VEGETABLE OIL
1 EGG
2 CUPS FLOUR
2/3 CUP SUGAR
1/8 CUP MOLASSES
1/2 TEASPOON BAKING SODA

EAT YOURSELF OR SHARE WITH YOUR HORSE.

MIX ALL INGREDIENTS TOGETHER. POUR INTO GREASED
AND FLOURED INSERT. PLACE ON 3 BALLS OF ALUMINUM
FOIL UNDER INSERT.

COOK ON HIGH 4-6 HOURS.

Care, and not fine stables, makes a good horse.
~Danish Proverb

OATS & PEPPERMINT

1 CUP OATS
3 TABLESPOONS WHEAT FLOUR
1/2 CUP APPLE JUICE
1 TEASPOON BROWN SUGAR
1 APPLE, CORED & DICED
8-10 PEPPERMINTS CRUSHED

MIX ALL INGREDIENTS THOROUGHLY, POUR INTO GREASED
& FLOURED INSERT. PLACE ON 3 BALLS OF ALUMINUM
FOIL TO ALLOW AIR FLOW.

COOK ON LOW 4-6 HOURS, HIGH NOT RECOMMENDED

Horseback riding is life, the rest is just details.
~Anonymous

OAT CARROT CAKE

1 CUP OATS
1/2 CUP CARROT JUICE
1/3 CUP MOLASSES
1 TABLESPOON HONEY
3 CARROTS, SHREDDED
1 CUP FLOUR

COMBINE ALL INGREDIENTS. POUR INTO GREASED AND FLOURED INSERT, PLACE IN SLOW COOKER ON 3 ALUMINUM FOIL BALLS.

COOK ON LOW 4-6 HOURS, HIGH NOT RECOMMENDED

It excites me that no matter how much machinery replaces the horse, the work it can do is still measured in horsepower.... even in this space age. And although a riding horse often weighs half a ton, and a big drafter a full ton, either can be led about by a piece of string if he has been wisely trained. This to me is a constant source of wonder, and challenge. ~Margaret Henry

Peanut Butter Yumm

1 cup oats
1 cup apple juice
1/2 cup creamy peanut butter
1/2 cup whole wheat flour
1 apple, cored, chopped fine

Combine all ingredients into greased and floured insert. Place on 3 aluminum balls in slow cooker to allow air flow.

Cook on low 4-6 hours.

I live in a house, but my home is in the stable.
~Anonymous

Apple Molasses Treats

4-6 APPLES, CORED, CUT IN HALF
2 TABLESPOONS HONEY
1 TABLESPOON MOLASSES
1/2 CUP OATS
2 TABLESPOONS WATER

POUR WATER INTO SLOW COOKER. PLACE APPLES INSIDE.
DRIZZLE HONEY AND MOLASSES OVER THE APPLES. TOP
WITH OATS.

COOK ON LOW 2-4 HOURS

Nothing is more sacred as the bond between a horse and a rider. No other creature can ever become so emotionally close to a human as a horse. When a horse dies, the memory lives on, because an enormous part of his owner's heart, soul, and the very existence dies also. ~Stephanie M. Thorn

Slow Cooker Tips:

- When purchasing a slow cooker, I prefer a programmable one. This allows me to set the amount of time for cooking; then the slow cooker turns to warm automatically. Remember food continues to cook when the slow cooker is set on the warm mode, so adjust cooking time accordingly.

- On most slow cookers, the setting for low is 200 degrees, high is 300; however, this can vary according to the brand you purchase. Check the manual or contact the manufacturer for more information. Cooking times will vary from slow cooker to slow cooker. If the recipes in this book cause your dishes to become over or under cooked, please assume that you will need to adjust the cooking times throughout the book to accommodate your slow cooker.

- To sear in flavors or reduce fat, it is recommended that meats be browned before placing in the slow cooker.

- To avoid harmful bacteria, hamburger should be browned before placing in slow cooker.

- Every time the lid is removed while cooking, thirty minutes of cook time is lost.

- Always add dairy products in the last thirty minutes to an hour of cooking time, to avoid curdling.

- To keep vegetables crisper, add them the last thirty minutes to one hour to of cook time.

- To clean slow cooker, soak ceramic liner in soapy water, and use a non-abrasive cleaning pad to avoid scratching the liner. For stains, add warm water and 2 cups of vinegar or 3 tablespoons of baking soda. Turn to low and let soak overnight. Scrub with hot soapy water, rinse and dry.

- When using an insert, choose a glass or metal pan that fits easily in the slow cooker. Do not fill more than half full. Lift it off of the bottom by placing 3 to 4 rolled balls of aluminum foil underneath. Air must be able to circulate in order for food to cook. You can contact a manufacturer to purchase an insert with a lid. Cooking time will vary according to which type of insert is used.

- Elevation should be considered when using the slow cooker.

- If you use a slow cooker that is not programmable, one way to avoid having food get overcooked is to purchase a programmable timer from a hardware store. The timer will then turn the slow cooker on and off at designated times.

With every purchase,
a donation is made to one of these fine charities:

Animal Welfare Institute
900 Pennsylvania Ave., SE Washington, DC
20003

Compton Jr. Posse
"Keeping Kids on Horses and Off the Streets"
Mayisha Akbar
Executive Director
453 W. Caldwell St.
Compton, CA 90220

Neigh Savers Foundation, Inc.
1547 Palos Verdes Mall, Suite 259
Walnut Creek, CA 94597-2228